STEADY &
TREMBLING

STEADY & TREMBLING

Art, Faith, & Family in an Uncertain World

TOM MONTGOMERY-FATE

For Dan,
a dear friend
and treasured
colleague –

CHALICE
PRESS

ST. LOUIS, MISSOURI

Cover art: Tom Montgomery-Fate and Karen Johnson
Cover and interior design: Elizabeth Wright
Interior art: Tom Montgomery-Fate, pages 1, 3, 67, 119;
      Karen Johnson, pages 37, 39, 65, 89, 91

Visit Chalice Press on the World Wide Web at
www.chalicepress.com

10 9 8 7 6 5 4 3 2 1   05 06 07 08 09 10

Library of Congress Cataloging–in–Publication Data

Montgomery-Fate, Tom.
  Steady and trembling : art, faith, and family in an uncertain world /
Tom Montgomery-Fate.
    p. cm.
  ISBN-10: 0-827234-65-1 (pbk. : alk. paper)
  ISBN-13: 978-0-827234-65-9
  1. Montgomery-Fate, Tom. 2. Christian life. I. Title.
  BR1725.M525A5 2005
  242—dc22

                                         2005013222

Printed in the United States of America

For
Carol, Tessa, Abby, and Bennett

Contents

Foreword

This is a book about epiphanies of light. It also is about the starless night that rides above America. Tom Montgomery-Fate's reflections on how we create and are created offer absolution—the freedom to lose our way. He writes from darkness against darkness. All we have, he insists, is each other and eyes for the light that is breaking up ahead.

So much obscures our vision. Tom struggles to discern the revelation of the natural world that lies hidden in plain sight. He writes as a husband who is often confused, as a father broken open by his children's fragility and courage, and as an artist startled by the beauty of dusk rising in the open fields. Most critically, he writes of his search for the silence that asks nothing, but opens the heart of the world.

These extraordinary essays on art, family, and faith are divided into the four seasons, each of which Tom searches for the miracle of ordinary wisdom: in the barren death of a goldfinch, in the resurrection of wildflowers in the meadow, in the raccoons that *"waddle through the forsythia like furry tanks,"* and in his son's birth, a moment of *"both separation and union, of both leaving and arriving home."*

Tom writes from a henhouse sitting on the edge of a meadow two miles from Lake Michigan. There he snatches weekend retreats away from a Chicago suburb with its domesticated quietude. In Michigan he waits, watching ruby-throated hummingbirds and red-tailed hawks, noticing white-tailed does and turtledoves silhouetted against sunset's canopy. His only method for bearing the weight of the world's suffering and incomprehensibility is his willingness to be present. He tells us his purpose:

> I want to live on the cusp of the material and immaterial. I don't want to understand the universe in the usual way—to compartmentalize and measure it or prove it exists—but to belong to it: awake and aware, connected to the sunlight, water, air, and the heat that created me, that creates all life. This search for connection is a prayer.

The search is through cultural darkness and confusion, and not knowing the way forward. Tom Montgomery-Fate surrenders to doubt about himself as a writer, a parent, and a person who "knows" what is to be done to staunch the world's great wounds. He sees the cartography of our losses as openings to our true human condition. Thus, the search for certainty, for the flawless, is a kind of death for the artist and for the parent who risks faith in human freedom. *"Art requires discomfort and vulnerability. It does not lead toward perfection but away from it. Not toward the ideal, but the human."*

Faith in the human strips. It is why Tom and his wife and companion, Carol, have sought the courage of peasants in Nicaragua and the Philippines. Among the dispossessed they surrendered the burden and illusion of dominion. It is not only the artist's risk of creativity that Tom pursues but the risk of solidarity alongside those with frail protection and uncommon hope. It was the poor persons of Nicaragua and the Philippines who helped teach the Montgomery-Fates the art of "failing."

Over and over, Tom takes up the task of faith in the face of doubt and terror. The reader enters a Pine Ridge sweat lodge with Tom, searching for Wanka Tanka, the great spirit. Tom is not a "brave," but a man afraid of suffocating confinement. Yet he enters the rock-hissing womb because he trusts the Lakota elders who guide him. It is this surrender of control that opens Tom to the whole and holy Presence that surrounds us. Exiting the sweat lodge, Tom sees the world anew and his place in it:

> There on the frozen cusp of the Dakota plains, I stood under a dome of flickering stars and watched the soft fingers of moonlight reaching for the barren trees, for the mirror of the frozen creek, and for us. And I wondered if I ever felt so small, or like I knew so little, or so deeply connected to the whole.

Tom's language, lush and poetic, is also precise. He uses words to arrive at a place beyond words. This is his sacred task—to speak of the elusive, ever-present Mystery that surrounds us. Yet he recognizes the impossibility of language describing the mystery of our own complex restlessness and sacred longings. He is trying, as Teilhard de

Chardin once said, "to go a little beyond the frontier of sensible appearances in order to see the divine."

In the end the book is an open invitation to the radical simplicity of attention, of embracing awe.

RENNY GOLDEN,
Northeastern Illinois University,
author of *The Hour of the Furnaces* and *War on Families*

Acknowledgments

Thanks to the following journals in which these essays appeared (sometimes in a revised form and with different titles): "Falling," in *Across Cultures: A Reader for Writers* (New York: Pearson Longman, 6th ed., originally in *Mothering*); "Homing," "Steady and Trembling," and "Something Enormous" in *Puerto Del Sol* (Las Cruces, N.M.: New Mexico State Univ.); "Making Time," in *Mothering* (Santa Fe, N.M.); "Henhouse" and "Perfectly Flawed," in *The Other Side* (Philadelphia). ("Perfectly Flawed" was originally a talk given at Calvin College's Festival of Faith and Writing.)

Thanks to these editors for their honesty and kindness: Ashisha, Sheena Gillespie, Gail Lavendar, Monica Torres, Dee Dee Risher, Doug Davidson, and Aina Barten.

Thanks to National Public Radio's "Living on Earth" show and Chicago Public Radio's "848" show, where excerpts from "Henhouse Prayer," "Falling," "Creatures," "Homing," "Enough," "Spider," "The Nature of Violence," and "On Saving the World" aired. And thanks to those editors: Eileen Bolinsky (National Public Radio) and Cate Cahan (Chicago Public Radio).

Thanks to Carol Montgomery-Fate for carefully reading both the print and the person behind it, for her patience, and for giving me the gift of time. She encouraged and enabled the solitude I needed to do much of this writing.

Thanks to Bill, Byron, Deborah, Susan, Renny, and Roberta from our "nice" writers group. Their insight and encouragement often kept me going.

Thanks to Cindy Crosby, a remarkably generous writer, for her botanical expertise and for helping me believe in work I was unsure of.

Thanks to Karen Johnson, botanical artist, for permission to use her lovely artwork. (http://www.science-art.com/member.asp?id=30)

Thanks to Bob Dixon-Kolar, David McGrath, and Susan Messer for their editing suggestions.

Thanks to my friend Dan Dale for the hours of walking, talking, and working together on the farm. Thanks to Nancy Jones for writing a history of the farm. And thanks to all the other farm members who supported this endeavor: Jim and Juanita Burris, Jean and Don Ervin, Dan and Sharon Hunter-Smith, Parker Quammen and Sheila Boss, Sara Pitcher, Jay and Pat Wilcoxin, (and in memory of two of the farm's founders: Alvin Pitcher and Judith Arlene Mitchell).

Thanks to Wendolyn Tetlow, Sheryl Mylan, and Jan Geesaman at the College of DuPage, for their interest, insight, and support of this work.

Thanks to the Ragdale Foundation for two residencies to focus on this book.

Thanks to these core mentors: Carl Klaus, Richard Lloyd-Jones, David Wilson, and Cleo Martin (who passed away shortly after I began work on this book).

Thanks to the editors/staff at Chalice Press for their support and insight: Trent Butler, Pam Brown, Susie Burgess, Lynne Letchworth, Sarah Tasic, Kristin Westphal, Elizabeth Wright (and in memory of Jane McAvoy, former editorial director).

And finally, thanks to my parents, Russ and Dee Fate, and to my three older brothers—Kendall, Paul, and Robin—for loving and living with such passion, and giving me so much to believe in.

Quo Vadis

Sometimes I choose a cloud and let it
cross the sky floating me away.
Or a bird unravels its song and carries me
as it flies deeper and deeper into the woods.
Is there a way to be gone and still
belong? Travel that takes you home?
Is that life?—to stand by a river and go.

—WILLIAM STAFFORD

AUTUMN

*Autumn teaches us that fruition is also death; that
ripeness is a form of decay. Leaves are verbs that
conjugate the seasons.*

—Gretel Ehrlich[1]

Henhouse Prayer

Why should I wish to see God better than this day?
—WALT WHITMAN[2]

Night struggles toward day. A soft band of peach light brightens the horizon, lends a faint blueness to the sky, turns the darkness into a silhouette of distant trees, creates a landscape. Chimney swifts dart and dip in the new light. As it gathers into a glowing ball, it burns away the low clouds of mist hanging on the meadow and filters through a stand of pines and oaks, just a few feet from my door.

I'm sitting in the henhouse, waiting for words. The east end of this long, low, shacklike structure is screened in and opens to a fifty-acre plot of meadow and woods—the cooperative farm to which my family belongs. Five families from our old church on Chicago's south side purchased this farm in southwest Michigan twenty-five years ago. It's a retreat from the smog and wail of sirens, the endless grid of concrete and cars just ninety minutes away. Here there are two-lane roads rather than eight, local fruit stands rather than strip malls, and the entire shining dome of the sky rather than the slivers of sunlight that slip though the city walls of glass and steel.

Those families came here wanting less to own a piece of the natural world than to belong to it. They dug out a half-acre garden, rebuilt the main house (which was destroyed by fire), carved a network of walking trails through the back woods, and filled a fallow 40-acre soybean field by planting nearly a thousand oak and pine trees. That field is now a young forest. The straight white pines, which served as stakes for the red oaks, are now ready to be cut. The oaks need to be thinned.

The henhouse is primitive, but comfortable. On one side the ceiling is four feet high, but it quickly slants up to 6' 2". Though I am 6' 1", the clearance is somehow more calming than claustrophobic, a good fit. The interior is a montage of rummage sale discoveries: a maroon shag carpet remnant that covers the cracked concrete foundation, an orangey-brown flowered couch, a tilty full-sized pool table, and a rusted-out pot belly stove. There is electricity but no water. Yet, hidden behind a curtain door near the entrance is a narrow closet-like bathroom. The wooden box commode has a removable plastic pot. Over the "sink" (a tin pan and a gallon jug of water) is a cracked medicine cabinet mirror that still has a $1.00 sticker on it.

The exterior is bright barn red. A half-dozen wasp nests and two abandoned bird nests cling to the soffits. Most of the salvaged aluminum screens don't fit the windows and are simply nailed into the wood to cover the openings. I plug the small holes in the screens with wads of toilet paper, a trick I learned while living in the Philippines. Even so, the mosquitoes and gnats find a way in. A half-dozen ladybugs land on my computer screen and are marching across these words as I type. I let them be. They live here. I am the outsider.

At 20 by 40 feet, the henhouse is too large to be a "cell," a term artists use to highlight isolation and authenticate suffering, to evoke prisons and monasteries. I seek what the monk and the artist seek: the time and space to create and to be created. But I have no illusions. This is not a "hermit goes to the woods, eats roots and berries, finds enlightenment" kind of story. Rather, it is a search for the words that might find something holy in an ordinary life, in any ordinary life. Bushes are burning everywhere.

My wife Carol and I have three young children. So my solitude is irregular, impure, and a rare gift. My stays are often short and always unpredictable. Yet the movement between a busy family and work life in a Chicago suburb, and the slow deliberate life alone here on the edge of a patch of woods is instructive. It fills me with confusion, and joy. I feel lost, yet at home. And oddly, my brief stays here are beginning to feel less like a retreat from my family than a journey back to them.

Today I taped a quote from the French mystic Simone Weil on the bottom of the plastic frame of my computer screen: "Attentiveness without an aim is the supreme form of prayer."[3] This is why I come here: to pray, to listen for the quiet warble of creation.

Openings

A hard rain late last night raised the worms. A golden flicker snatches one from the weeds and flaps off toward a cottonwood tree with the wriggling night crawler clamped in its beak. I listen to the buzz of the cicada swell and wane perhaps a dozen times, but soon I grow impatient. All morning my sentences have frayed and broken, unable to bear the awkward weight of my thoughts.

By noon a gale blows in from Lake Michigan, which lies two miles to the west. The gusts break up the sky, tearing small holes in a thin, gray blanket of cloud. I walk outside to watch these openings cut sudden, translucent sleeves of sunlight that illuminate patches of dried grass and twisted brambles far below on the meadow. As the gaps in the clouds change shape, the light grows, diminishes, disappears, or appears afresh elsewhere—abruptly throwing a crimson stand of staghorn sumac into brilliant relief. A patch of wild parsnips and goldenrod suddenly appear at the base of one of the soft, luminous tubes. It all seems so random. The sumac, the parsnips, the goldenrod had always been there. But now, bathed in the warm channel of light, they become something new—a single, glowing moment. As I scratch out these details with a blue ballpoint pen on a yellow legal pad, the delicate shifting blotches of light on the meadow remind me how art works, of the stunning, fragile quality of inspiration, of creation.

Thirty years ago, as a seventh grader, I was trying to write a description of a walk in a snowstorm on an Iowa country road when I first felt it—how the pages and pages of my thick words drifting through a spiral notebook could somehow open, throwing the world into a startling new light. Back then I didn't consider words sacred, nor writing an art, but I was hooked on something that I still seek—in books, in painting, in music, at church, or at the dinner table—everywhere. At thirteen, I didn't know that art is not only a form of communication but a *communion,* that when the reader or viewer encounters art, she too stands in that miraculous shaft of light that the artist has noticed and shared. Nor did I know that the light of the creation is filtered through the beholder's experience, that art is made more complex and intricate because it is re-created in each reading or viewing. All I knew that winter in Maquoketa, Iowa, was that the snowstorm was howling on that two-dimensional surface, that my feet were scrunching ice and gravel in the ink and paper.

I stare back out at the meadow. Things are just starting to die, to dry out. Soon they will fall apart and blow away. The Queen Anne's lace has begun to close into the tiny green bowls my daughters like to pretend are miniature bird nests, or chic, earthy hats for their Barbies. In a week they will collapse into tinier brown fists.

About half of the leaves are still green. The cottonwood turned first. Some of the brown, brittle-veined hearts have already made their short flight to the earth, scattered in the wind, and settled somewhere to decay. The silver maples are the last to go. Sometimes raw green-and-red patches dapple the same leaf, making visible the continuity of life and death.

Today I am dreaming of that cycle, of those moments of transition, of fall freezing into winter, of winter melting into spring. I am dreaming of how the April sun will filter through the barren trees and find the dormant flowers lining the oxbow beyond the meadow— the bloodwort, trillium, and Solomon's seal. How it will slowly awaken and raise them, ending their long crouch in the muddy weeds and shadow. I am dreaming of what light can do.

I look up from my legal pad to watch a red-tailed hawk drop off its perch on an oak limb into a teetering glide, skim over the treetops, climb into a thermal, and kite back toward me. The sky has abruptly changed, now half empty, half blue. In full sun the meadow is relit into a dried sea of early autumn colors. Sumac and parsnips and goldenrod are again part of the whole. The magical spotlights have disappeared. They only lasted a moment. No one can intentionally create one of these transcendent moments, one of these openings to the light in all things, so I search for ways to be ready, to attend.

Religion scholar Huston Smith writes that sunlight is an inherent link between spirituality and science: "Light creates. It pumps power into the spatio–temporal world. The immaterial light flowing from the sun is transformed into the earth's green carpet of vegetation. Because photons of light are situated on the cusp of the material and immaterial, they are not subject to our usual ways of understanding the universe."[4]

I want to live on the cusp of the material and immaterial. I don't want to understand the universe in the usual way—to compartmentalize and measure it or prove it exists—but belong to it: awake, aware, connected to the sunlight, water, air, and the heat that created me, that creates all life. This search for connection is a prayer.

Steady and Trembling

"Reason explains the darkness, but it is not a light."

—Noah ben Shea[5]

As I walk back to the henhouse, dozens of grasshoppers chaotically lunge for safety, always just a few feet ahead of each step I take. They tick in the grass like new rain. I sit down at my desk and begin to sort through my "seeds" file—a collection of photos and poems I turn to when the words stop coming. I find Howard Nemerov's poem "Trees." He writes that trees are "steady as a rock and always trembling" and that they "stand for the constant presence of process." The biggest trees send down the deepest and widest root-line. But no matter the strength of that anchor, the new growth, the tender branches and raw green leaves, are always vulnerable to the weather, to the indifferent, shifting winds. In a storm they survive by bending.

A life in art is also "steady and trembling"—an unpredictable, illogical pursuit of connection, of relation, with self and family and the whole of creation, while trying to live in the "constant presence of process." Yet while I understand the trembling part, I'm still unsure how to steady myself in a three-child, two-job, too busy, high-expectation "normal" life; in an ever-accelerating, ultra-compartmentalized, 24/7 world, where success is increasingly defined by productivity and accessibility, where to slow down is to lose or fail. Our creative search for meaning—for connection with our children, our partners, God— must compete with our "to do" lists, with the lure of money, with the lie that we can buy back the time we have already squandered to our hectic schedules and the ever-expanding dream of economic security.

The problem is that when we download our lives on a palm planner, the preprogrammed beeps, the digitized "mind," leads us only into the future, rather than the *presence* we seek. In a world of "never-enoughness," we often miss the gaps in the clouds, the openings, those apertures of meaning that would light the way.

A thesaurus lists *creative* as a synonym for *productive*, but not *productive* as a synonym for *creative*. Productivity may require creativity, but the opposite is not true. And while these words are sometimes used interchangeably, we associate productivity with commodification and measurement. A product comes at the end of a process, as a result, while a creation may still be in process, unfinished, evolving. We equate productivity with the bottom-line world of business, and creativity with the bottomless world of art. We don't have a "Gross National Creation," or name God as "The Producer."

I am *un*steady and trembling. The insecurity and ambiguity of the process of art means that I can't always know if I'm at beginning or end—just starting, or almost done—when or how or where the sun will find its way through the clouds. This can prompt self-doubt and guilt: What am I *doing* here in the henhouse? How could I put such a burden on my family? What do I have to show for this time? Do eight or nine good sentences constitute a full day's work?

"Writing a novel is like a driving a car at night," writes E. L. Doctorow. "You can only see as far as the headlights, but you can make the whole trip that way."[6] Focus on what you can see from where you are, on what's close to you. Don't worry that the headlights could go out, that the engine could die, that the road could turn in an unfamiliar direction. *The journey is home.* For me, this is where the arts of writing, faith, and family seem to intersect.

All are a process of discovery. The work can be enthralling and ecstatic, or lonely and confusing. It is full of detours. This piece of writing itself is an essay, stemming from the Latin root *essai,* which means "trial" or "attempt." A successful writer simply keeps attempting to write. A successful religious faith is a perpetual attempt to believe, to love what you cannot always comprehend. Successful parents just keep attempting to love their children, who are brimming with joy and rage, with blind trust and raw fear. A successful marriage epitomizes *essai*—a constant attempt to find meaning amid the dull and stunning routines of a committed relationship.

Kurt Vonnegut claims that when he writes he feels "like an armless legless man with a crayon in his mouth."[7] This image of unpreparedness, of disability, seems like comic exaggeration, yet it is also often how I feel when I try to create, to write or pray or parent. Art requires discomfort and vulnerability. It does not lead toward perfection, but away from it. Not toward the ideal, but toward the *human*.

"Ring the bells that can still ring, " writes Leonard Cohen. "Forget your perfect offering. There's a crack in everything. That's how the light gets in."[8] A supposed flaw or failing is often the catalyst of artistic expression, a point of access to creation.

I look up from my desk to see a wounded house wren circle out of the light flooding on the meadow, glide toward me, and abruptly begin to flounder. The four ounces of blood and feather flap desperately against the wind, before trying to emergency-land on a quivering black limb near the top of a 50-foot silver maple tree. It hits the moving target but can't hold and falls like a startled promise— three seconds of beating a thousand bits of sky into hopelessness. The earth soars up to catch and crush it.

House wrens have remarkably intricate skeletons. A tiny bone somewhere must have cracked—the hairline of weakness making flight impossible. Then the end comes—the death flutter in the weeds, which attracts a cat. The delighted tabby slinks back toward the shed with the warm, still-twitching body stuffed in his mouth.

The bird's sudden tumble reminds me of a friend whose wife just left him and their child, unexpectedly, for someone new. "I'm not angry," he says on the phone, "Just unbelievably sad." The tiny, barely known, essential "bones" that sometimes snap in everyone's life— that throw us into emotional tailspins—are so minute that the breaks sometimes aren't evident for months, or years. And they can happen anywhere:

– while chatting with colleagues in the office about movies or war or property values,
– while idling in a line of honking cars on the expressway,
– while trying to spoon mashed bananas into a defiant child's closed mouth, or
– while frantically searching for a wad of lost keys, a misplaced billfold, or the quiet courage to start over.

I worry about my friend. What was he thinking that day he discovered her infidelity? What thoughts drifted through his brain that night in bed, while Jay Leno was laughing and he was lying next to someone he didn't know? After fifteen years of trying to make a marriage and a family work, of mending breaks, I wonder if he can recover in midair and find a place to land.

In framing the bird's last moment, and the last days of my friend's marriage, I rely on the only method I have for making sense of the world, for composing a life in art: pay attention. Artists don't frame moments to change them, but to change the beholder, and themselves. Attending to the seemingly mundane details in daily life is what opens me to the sacred—to how the house wren and my estranged friend are both broken and beautiful.

I understand this intellectually, but as I watch the meadow in the soft brush of late afternoon light, I again become unsure. A maroon maple leaf, twisted and loosened by the wind, slowly spirals to the ground. A white-tailed doe, her summer coat already darkening and thickening as winter approaches, tentatively walks near the trailhead. She cocks her head in the direction of an unfamiliar sound or scent and bolts into the woods, her body crashing through the thicket.

The question returns. I can't shake it. What am I doing here? Is it all right to be creative but not productive? Does art really matter? Every artist I know struggles with doubt.

A guilty elbow of responsibility keeps nudging my conscience. I should be home with Carol, washing dishes or folding laundry, or reading books to our young daughters, or changing our two-year-old's diaper, or revising a syllabus, or replacing that rotten fascia behind our leaky gutter. Instead, I have been sitting here for three days watching, listening, waiting.

Yesterday morning I discovered something about the thousands and thousands of dew beads that hang precariously from the tips of every white pine needle in the woods. If they are not disturbed, they never fall to the ground. Rather, by midday, they evaporate in the sunlight. In dozens of previous walks through the woods, I never noticed this.

I stare at clouds and deer and trees for hours, yet I am not a meteorologist or biologist or botanist. I have friends who are now preparing to do civil disobedience at the School of the Americas, a military training school in Fort Benning, Georgia. Other friends are struggling to live and teach in rural Mexico, and still others grow sixty-five species of organic fruits and vegetables in their own backyard. What am I doing here?

As dusk approaches, the only answer I can ever muster rises slowly on a breath from my lungs to my mind: *writing, like all art, is an act of faith in creation.*

The natural light in my room dims, and the sharp lines of shadow soften. I put my legal pad away, pull on a sweatshirt, and walk to the edge of the meadow and sit down. The sky is thickening in the west. Clouds darken and sink behind the trees. But the northern sky is still breaking up into a drifting gray and white puzzle—soft, billowing pieces that fit anywhere. There, along a split rail fence line, a lone sycamore tree, raging with crows, looms over the meadow. It blows and bends and waits. Deeply rooted, rock-steady at the center, the tender limbs and trembling green and yellow leaves continue to grow toward the fleeting light.

Falling

Our human problem—one common to parents, sons, and daughters—is letting go while holding tight to the unraveling yarn that ties our hearts.

—Louise Erdrich[9]

Late this morning I reread May Sarton's essay, "The Rewards of Living a Solitary Life." "Alone one is never lonely,"[10] she claims, distinguishing between physical and psychological separation. My freshman composition students like this line and quote it in their papers. They say things like, "I have felt 'lonely' at big parties surrounded by people," or, "I feel most 'alone,' when I'm not pushed, or distracted." But some also feel that Sarton is too removed, a bit odd, a little unbalanced. My student Joan, a single mother, wrote, "She doesn't live in the real world. I work full-time and have two toddlers. Most of us can't even dream about 'alone' time. It's too painful."

Early afternoon. After three days of writing in the henhouse I feel empty—not a calming Zen-like emptiness, but confusion, a loneliness that even the rustle of the silver maples and a handful of ripe sand cherries can't heal.

Depression, a familiar veil of darkness, is drifting from my head to my heart when our minivan crunches down the gravel drive. I'm elated to see Carol and the kids, and to return home tonight. They bring lunch. We eat peanut butter sandwiches and Granny Smith apples in the grassy shade of the henhouse. Soon our daughters, Tessa and Abby, wander over to the garage and swing open the half-rotten wooden doors to find the rusted tangle of a half-dozen old bicycles inside. They look for ones they can ride. So do Carol and I. The tires are low, the chains loose. There are no helmets and no attached seat for Bennett, our two-year-old son. We decide to go to the beach instead.

But the bikes, the tools hanging everywhere from sixpenny nails, and the damp, oily smell remind me of our own garage and our own pile of used bikes and trikes and scooters. As I buckle Bennett's wriggling body into his car seat, I wonder when I will teach him to ride. I ask him if he would like to learn. He gives his emphatic one word response to any question we ask this month: "No!" He wildly shakes his head back and forth to drive the point home.

I think of past years, when I taught the girls to ride on the jogging trail near our home. The memories steady me. The last riding lesson I remember was a few years ago—in late spring. The trail had again turned from a frozen dirt path through a silhouette of trees and brambles into a leafy green tunnel. Smartweed, nettles, and sassafras sprang from the warming earth. Overhead, new leaves defined a network of elm and oak branches, which blocked most of the light. The wooden frame homes that line the path had disappeared behind the swaying walls of green. We could no longer see around the trail's frequent bends and turns. But it was a comforting blindness, one I looked forward to.

Abby was still in love with her red trike, and skeptical of taking on Tessa's old two-wheeler with training wheels. The bike was a little too big for her, the seat a little too high, even in its lowest position. The gritty bearings made pedaling difficult, and the training wheels were rust-locked a bit out of position. Tessa had a new bike and was zooming all around us, chattering encouragement to her younger sister. When I first lifted Abby onto the seat and she tried to pedal, she was worried. It felt too "tippy." Determined, she got back on and practiced. As she slowly cranked the wheels forward and rolled down the path, she began to lean her torso and shift her shoulders when the bike began to tip. Soon, she found her balance.

That night at supper Tessa recalled her own fear when she first rode a two-wheeler. Like Abby, she didn't trust that the training wheels would "catch her." But what I most remember is when we took the training wheels off. Over and over I sprinted behind Tessa down the path with my hand on the small of her back as she pedaled and coasted and wobbled and dipped. It was awkward because I was both slightly pushing her forward and trying to hold her up—wanting to both keep her going and keep her from falling. As I panted along behind, I encouraged her and reiterated two instructions: "Keep the handlebars straight," and, "Don't shift your butt in the seat." Her face was screwed so tightly in concentration that I don't know if she heard. She was listening more to her body—to what it knew about balance, to what it feels like to roll upright into the wind on two thin rubber tires in spite of gravity. Seeing her focus, I stopped talking, other than an occasional, "You're doing great!" She didn't say a word after the first few attempts. Though, when she finally fell in the dirt, she looked up at me like I had let her down. I consoled her, inspected her scrapes, and then said what my Dad had said: "Get right back on. You can do it!" After a half-dozen more attempts she could nearly balance herself. Then she began to say it. The same thing I said to my Dad.

"Let go!" "Let go!"

I finally did. She abruptly veered off the path onto a connected sidewalk, careened off someone's picket fence, bumped through their front yard, dodged a tangled garden hose, slowed her bike, and gently fell into a forsythia bush. I walked over to find her laughing.

When I tell this story to my friend Ken, a psychologist, he explains physical balance, how it works: Neurons in Tessa's inner ear are constantly firing to monitor her body's position and movement in space. "We learn it only by doing," Ken says. "The hands teach the brain." Once you learn how, you never forget. It's called kinethesis—a primitive, survival behavior—something we share with monkeys and dogs. Psychological balance, however, is much harder to define, and more elusive.

I wish parenting was like riding a bike, or taping drywall, or playing a *C* scale on the piano—something you could master and remember. But once you learn how, you always forget, because the "how" keeps changing. Coasting is rare. Pedaling uphill into the wind isn't: Fatigue grows into a roaring tantrum. Scissors are the only solution to a grape bubble-gum hairball. It's five minutes too late to replace the permanent set of markers with the washable ones. A Barbie's head gets "accidentally" flushed down the toilet and is jammed somewhere inside the porcelain gooseneck.

Dan, a founding member of this farm, used to take his daughters for rides on their tandem bike through the Michigan countryside. When they were small, Dan rode in front so he could steer. But as Jenny and Lucy grew older, they grew tired of their father's wide back and head blocking their view of the vineyards and wildflowers. They wanted to control the bike themselves, to take their father for a ride rather than vice versa. So Dan moved to the rear. As his girls guided him along the bumpy gravel lanes he noticed that they pedaled slower than he did and were less concerned about their destination. Still tall enough to see where they were going, he learned to enjoy riding in back. And the bike was more stable with his greater bulk in the rear position.

Bonnie, one of my former teachers, remembers when her son, Chris, first learned to ride a bike. After several practice sessions, he still couldn't quite balance himself. Then early one morning, while dressing, Bonnie and her husband looked out their bedroom window to see Chris riding all alone on the front sidewalk. As he triumphantly wobbled by, he turned to look up at them. "I don't need you anymore," he yelled in a moment of joy.

Sometimes I dream of not being needed, or of being needed a lot less. I dream of the day our kids will learn to balance themselves so well that they will all ride away and only come back to visit—with college degrees, meaningful jobs, interesting partners, and perhaps a child laughing or crying in the back seat. But my deeper hope is that they will learn to not fear falling. That they will risk. That they will follow what they love and believe it can lead them where they need to go.

Some nights I lie awake in bed next to Carol, long after she is asleep and the house has grown dark and still. I listen for the faint rhythms of our children breathing in their bedrooms, and I wonder how it is that they can both utterly confuse and completely sustain me. Freight trains rattle through the moonlit silhouettes of our little suburban town. Elm branches scratch at our wooden siding in the wind. My wind-up alarm clock steadily ticks on a cluttered nightstand. I start to remember things. Does it matter that I can't always tell whether these memories are from my childhood or theirs?

At times this blurring of our lives is all I have to right myself: We swashed brilliant grass-green paint across the bottom of white paper, swiped raw blue strokes of sky across the top, and floated a yellow sun ball in between. We concocted silly songs and knock-knock jokes while locked in a traffic jam. We hid in the forts we built from wet snow or dead limbs or blankets and chairs, delighting in the dark refuge. We buried hamsters and gerbils and turtles and goldfish, and had funeral services for each one. We played house and dress-up and pranced in the sprinkler and tried to count the stars. We flicked our wrists and watched a knot of worm fly out over the river, trailed by a red and white bobber and a double *kerplunk*. We learned to wait, to dream of the world beneath the moving water, to believe in the unseen.

Things didn't change as much as I thought they would during that long, bumpy ride from son to father. I am still my parents' child. I still struggle to fit in, and to stand out, and to feel at home somewhere. I still wonder if I am good enough, and fear I am missing something. I teeter on the wheels of instinct and reason, never quite in balance.

Sometimes I remember: a family, like faith, is not a problem to be solved, but an experiment in love. No matter the parent or the child or the bike or the street, we will fall—again and again—in sparkling sunlight, in hard rain, in bitter wind, in soft mud, and on unforgiving concrete. It's all about falling, and getting up, and trying again, or not. It's about the person that helped you up, or didn't. Or that you helped up, or didn't. But falling is not failing. Sometimes it feels like an opening, like what I fall into is the presence of God.

My own father just turned 80. Forty years ago he taught me how to ride a bike. I don't recall exactly how old I was or how many days it took me to learn. But I remember the bike: a little blue stingray with a vinyl banana seat. I remember the desperate struggle to stay upright, the falling, the startling joy of not falling. I remember a fantasy I shared with a friend: With enough raw downhill speed and the help of our unzipped coats snapping in the wind behind us, we could lift off the ground like the Wright brothers and pedal into the sky. I remember I trusted my father.

"You can do it," he said. More a promise than an expectation, these words were sometimes unspoken—a kind of faith, which I suppose told him when to let go of his four sons. I still hear those words now, as I run behind my children, gently pushing, trying to hold them up—along with myself. "You can do it," I say, listening to my father, and preparing to fall.

This afternoon when we arrive at the lake it seems much colder than at the farm. As we walk down the path to the beach in our shorts and T-shirts, Carol and I wish we had remembered sweaters. The kids are oblivious. They hear the surf before they see it, and tear off in a sprint. When they reach the lake, Bennett drops to his knees and begins to dig in the sand. After testing the chilly water with their toes, Tessa and Abby spill out the contents of their beach bag—three plastic buckets and shovels—and join Bennett. We all pack the pails with wet sand and tap them into little castles. Then we dig a hole large enough for Bennett to sit in and watch the walls cave in.

As Tessa and Abby keep playing, they notice the cold waves lapping at their feet less and less. Soon they wade in and begin diving into the troughs, pretending they are dolphins. But Bennett keeps his distance from the water, and not just because it is cold. A month ago while reaching over to pick up a red stone in the clear water beneath him, a wave bowled him over from behind. When I scooped him up, he coughed and sputtered before breaking into sobs of confusion. He still remembers. And the odd thing is that I do, too—both his tumble and mine. Decades ago, I was also baptized by this lake and rescued by my parents. I learned to love and fear the water on this same beach. I'm still learning.

After awhile Bennett grows tired of digging and waddles over to sit with Carol on our old blue blanket and eat crackers and watch his sisters play in the water. I also stop digging and watch the girls, who are now trying to body surf on the small waves. As they are lifted and dropped by the roll of the lake, I feel something lifting in me, something I have been fighting off all day, something dark and familiar that has a will of its own.

It is now, with my index finger, that I begin to trace the slightly curved raised lines that each wave forms as it pushes a film of sand up from the lake onto the shore: the wavelines. These thin, delicate ridges of sand string out along the beach in unending interlaced patterns, as if made by a family of water snakes in perpetual migration. Each line marks where a wave stopped and then receded back out into the lake. In their unending memory of the rhythm of the lake, the wavelines give me hope. They are the timeless moment of both arrival and departure, of ending and starting over, of falling and rising again and again, of the holy *then* that is *now*.

A Torn Map

*[E]ach must make a safe place of his heart, before so strange
and wild a guest as God approaches.*

—LI-YOUNG LEE[11]

This morning, in hopes of avoiding the Chicago rush "hour" (which lasts two or three hours), I leave Glen Ellyn for the farm at 6 a.m. The 290 inbound to the city is "open," meaning no gridlock, and I can at least keep moving. Still, it is an eight-lane weave among thousands of cars. The outbound is backed up—an accident. And the radio says I-55 south is at a standstill for a mile in both directions because a yelping, bewildered German shepherd is loose on the narrow grass median. Someone dumped him there. Gapers want to help but don't know how. I imagine the dog's panicked eyes—his fighting the instinct to run into the roar of interstate traffic toward the open land on the other side.

I reach the city center from the western 'burbs in a half hour and turn south on I-94. Soon I can see the bank clock that I used to read from the other side when we lived on the corner of 47th and Woodlawn: 70 degrees at 6:50 a.m.—odd weather for the first day of October. Yesterday it reached 78 degrees, a Chicago record for the

23

last day of September. The Robert Taylor Homes, a public housing high-rise, shoots out of the cracked concrete and abandoned storefronts beyond the 51st Street exit; then it's gone. Garfield Boulevard is next, the exit for The University of Chicago. A young mother cradling an infant on the second floor of a three-story apartment too close to the interstate leans out of her splintered window frame. She is close enough to smell the clouds of carbon rising from the gear-shifting semis as they roar by. Then I'm past her, but not her haunting presence.

Having grown up in Iowa, the city still overwhelms me. To my rural mind a million bodies packed into a few square miles can pull too tightly on the human braid of dream and desire, of suffering and joy, turning it, on a warm day, into a knot of disillusion that everyone would like to loosen a little, but has forgotten how.

Sick of the stench of exhaust, I close my window. At the moment the humming panel of glass locks in its rubber-cushioned frame, the honking and coughing engines are sealed out. My thoughts drift to my own family and old tapes start playing: Are these retreats into solitude irresponsible? Does my work warrant the sacrifice? Am I a good father and husband?

A line from my seeds file, which I read last night before bed, surfaces: "Creative work requires a loyalty as complete as the loyalty of water to the force of gravity." More Mary Oliver. I know what she means, but what about kids and groceries and vacuuming? How does one place "creative work" at the center of the "real world" that my student Joan (the overworked single mother) mentioned? Parenting is also "creative work," also art, but it's different—social rather than solitary, obligatory rather than elective. It's not an elaborate palette of colors for slow contemplation, but a wild and beautiful juggling act of love and loss, fear and hope.

All artists need a measure of personal freedom and self-confidence. But a parent's "freedom" may consist of the single hour that a toddler naps. And the emotional smorgasbord of a family inspires as much confusion as confidence. The "pull" of art outside of a family—of a poem, or a wet, spinning pot—always competes with the pull of obligation within a family—the ironing, soccer practice, a teacher conference.

Oliver, though she is not writing about the art of family or parenting, is right: The desire to let oneself fall headfirst into the solitary flow of creation is overwhelmingly powerful, like gravity. But it is not as predictable or reliable. And it can usually be resisted, or denied. What Oliver calls the artist's "loyalty" (which suggests clarity, even certainty), I call *faith*—in creation, in a Creator, and in myself as somehow related to both. Such a faith both sustains and confuses me. Yet, it is what I follow to Michigan, and what leads me back home again.

I'm learning to believe that the art of faith is the art of witness, of learning how to attend to life with imagination and *com-passion*— "suffering with" the world—tuning heart and head and hands to the creative work God offers. Poet-naturalist Patti Ann Rogers helps define this process with her idea of "reciprocal creation." For Rogers, creating art also re-creates the artist, making her both subject and object. "I realized…the power of my own creation to enter and alter my soul," she writes. "The language had created me."[12] From this spiritual center the artist can then claim her full *response ability*: "[O]ur obligations are mighty and humbling," Rogers writes. "We are cocreators. We are servants."[13] And for me, this service, this witness, is the work of praise, of gratitude.

Around 65th Street the El tracks run down the median of the highway. So in the innermost lane I'm fifteen feet from the train platform. Even at 70 miles per hour, I see men and women pacing and talking as they wait for their train. A girl in a red checkered dress playfully snatches the bill of a little boy's White Sox cap and runs off with it. The mother looks terrified that the kids will fall onto the tracks, and then I'm past them.

A half-hour later, a gray wall of cloud hanging behind the decaying steel mills along Lake Michigan in Gary, Indiana, becomes a mountain range on the horizon and conjures Wyoming. Then the sun unveils the truth: The distant mountains are floating in the middle of the lake and hiding a hundred belching smokestacks. But I'm still thankful for the quiet beauty sleeping everywhere. Here, even along the poisoned Calumet River, amid the stink of the tributary canals, are dozens of little elm and cottonwood trees, all reaching for the fire of the sun.

Just past Gary the traffic clogs. I fish out a map to check alternates, but it only includes the main veins—four-lane highways or bigger. The exit I want to try is backed up. I'm hesitant to take one of the exits not on the map. I have been lost before on such roads, on the network of narrow two-lanes that wind around the lake. The last time, I found myself driving through a string of bucolic vineyards at dusk and was so taken with the cool light and the rich, acrid smell of the earth that I just kept driving. I didn't realize I was heading south and east rather than north. I ended up in Pinhook, Indiana.

So today I keep inching along the toll way. But when I finally cross the border from Indiana into Michigan, I begin to lose my patience. An irritating twinge in my lower back radiates up my spine. I try to think of something hopeful and remember the mountain range of cloud. I concentrate on the image, and what it kindled in me, what I so often feel while whirring down the interstate between the rows of factories and soybean fields: Life is a rough draft, an imperfect gift; more a search for a direction than a destination. Maybe this is why I so often feel like I "arrive" while still on the road, while trying to navigate the crumpled, torn map of the heart.

Fleeting Light

*Nothing exists for its own sake but for a harmony greater than
itself which includes it. A work of art which accepts this
condition and exists upon its terms honors the creation and so
becomes a part of it.*

—Wendell Berry[14]

Today the sun rises behind a shifting bank of clouds, glowing
through the thinnest layers, but disappearing when they thicken.
When I start to review my calendar for the next week, obligations
spring up like weeds after a summer rain. They crowd out every quiet
thought. I trace the course of my breath for five or six cycles to recover
calm, then look down at my hands: blistered and scratched, stained
with sap and dirt. Last night I cut back the blackberry bushes and
split some elm logs. Physical labor centers me because, unlike with
writing, or teaching, or parenting, I know when I'm done, and what
I've done. For once, intention leads to completion: a neatly pruned
bush and a stack of wood to burn in the winter.

Art is less predictable. Less "seeing is believing" than believing in
seeing, in *revision*: viewing the subject again and again from the light
and shadow of perception. The blood-and-tissue camera called the

eye grows blurry less often than the eye of the mind, of interpretation and memory. Thus a poem or a painting may never feel finished. One simply chooses when to stop working on it. More work may feel abandoned than completed.

I walk outside. As a curtain of rain cloud sweeps by, a billowy seam gapes open for a moment and the sun bleeds through. Then the opening closes into a long, blue, drifting scar.

I think of a college mentor who recently died: Cleo. One spring morning in her office twenty years ago, she returned my reading journal, reviewed her comments, and then explained the next assignment—an observation essay. I asked for more direction. "Come to your senses," she said, finally. "And stay there." Cleo somehow turned a common reprimand into what felt like an affirmation, a gentle reminder for how to live—aware, connected.

By noon the sky is clear. Sometimes the pale cloudlessness comforts me. It looks like the inside of a bowl Carol made—the soft blue ceramic shine, the white flecks of sunlight all around me, defining my safe little niche on earth. But not today. The sky overwhelms rather than reassures: an infinite portal to the whole of creation as seen from my vantage point—a small animal squatting in a meadow, riding a planet, one of millions, on its hurtle through time.

I walk back to the henhouse, sift through my seeds file and find an excerpt from a Mary Oliver poem I scribbled down a few months ago.

> I don't know exactly what a prayer is.
> I do know how to pay attention, how to fall down
> into the grass, how to kneel down in the grass,
> how to be idle and blessed, how to stroll through the fields,
> which is what I have been doing all day.
> Tell me, what else should I have done?
> Doesn't everything die at last, and too soon?
> Tell me, what is it you plan to do
> with your one wild and precious life?[15]

Oliver's questions inspire and trouble me. The first feels rhetorical: *What else should I have done?* She knows the answer: nothing—except pay attention, except fall down where you are. But what if a dozen other "should haves" distract you? What if an argument or a missed deadline throws you off center and leaves you wobbling round and round in circles like a dented vase on a potter's wheel, waiting for someone or something to reform you?

"Wobbly" is my normal state. Maybe that's why, like Oliver, I don't hope to know "exactly" what a prayer is. Several days after I first read this poem I remember walking through the woods to the meadow beyond the creek and lying down amid the goldenrod and dragonflies. Somehow a wordless prayer rose out of me that day, into the grass and wind. And I wasn't thinking about it. It was less inquiry or invitation than surrender—to the gurgle of the creek, to some dove cooing nearby, and to fear, and loss, and all the questions I would never answer.

Oliver's second question also seems self-evident. Yes, everything dies. To live is to decay, to move toward death. The inevitable future is part of the unending now, which is all we have, and which is more than we can hold. Her final question plops this paradox and the haunting "should have" right back into our laps: "*What is it you plan to do?*" The only answer I can think of is "come to my senses."

When I sit back down at my computer, a black and yellow-striped body, with two long, dangling legs (landing gear) and a great dipping stinger, suddenly appears, hovering near the monitor. It drifts higher, then drops back toward me. I look over and spot a small hole in the screen about a foot from the grey comb of nest in the soffit. In menacing silence two more wasps drop through the screen into flight like stunned paratroopers. They seem as confused by their appearance inside the henhouse as I am. Four, then six, then nine more drop through. What is going on here?

I hear my mom's voice, and my own, to my kids: "Don't bother them, and they won't bother you." I don't want to kill them, but I can't ignore a full-scale attack. One makes a taunting orbit of my head. Another lands on my forearm. No sting. I brush him off and then prop the door open, trying to carefully shoo them out with a cushion from the couch. It doesn't work. Two new ones slink in through the open door. I close it and look for a good book—something thin and pliable with a durable cover. I try Thomas Merton's hardbound *Selected Poems* and trap one against the rusty, curved screen, but can't kill him. When I lift the book the wasp flies at me, lands in my hair. No sting. I swat him out of my hair and look for a thin, flexible volume, something with snap—Annie Dillard's *Holy the Firm*. This works. I kill four wasps in what I will claim was self-defense—smashing each segmented body against the wall or floor. Thankfully, the others slip back outside. I'm not sure how.

I duct tape over the hole in the screen, wipe off the little legs and sticky guts from the book cover, and then open it. I review my marginal notes, the lines I highlighted in college. Serendipity. Wasp-inspired research. I find no answers but some good questions—another way to think about what I'm doing here—battling wasps, watching birds die, and trying to determine the exact color of the sunrise. Dillard reflects on the nature of artistic creation:

> There is no such thing as an artist: there is only the world, lit or unlit as the light allows. When the candle is burning, who looks at the wick? When the candle is out, who needs it? But the world without light is wasteland and chaos…What can any artist set on fire but his world?[16]

I let these lines simmer. I walk outside with a pen and note pad and try to find some answers, perhaps some new words—hiding in the dripping grass, dangling from a silky strand of web, or buzzing around the red clover. A monarch hovers around a cone flower in a kind of flitting ballet, and then carefully sucks out a few drops of nectar. A poplar sapling slowly bends to and fro in the wind. Overhead, a broken V of honking geese reassemble themselves. High in the western sky, the geese cross over the slow curve of the earth, and under the sun, as it burns and burns and burns, creating the world again.

That night I dream I am riding my old Raleigh three speed on a gravel road in Iowa. No people or houses or cows or dogs—just the dusty line of the road, climbing and falling with the hills. The sun is sitting on the horizon, a golden ball on a green table, turning everything—field, sky, road—soft and shimmery. I desperately pump up and down hill after hill, but have no idea where I am going. I just know I have to get there soon. And then suddenly the sun ball slips beneath the horizon, leaving only a quivering silver thread

of light—enough to barely see the road beneath me, but not where I
am going. And then the sliver of light is gone. Darkness. The terror
of the dream is that I know that the sun will not return, that I have
just witnessed its final moments, and now, I will never arrive, never
discover my destination.

I bolt upright in sweaty confusion. When I realize it is night and
I was dreaming, I reach over and write a couple of sentences on the
notepad by my bed, and then fall back to sleep:

> Day and night, like life and death, are separated by an instant,
> by the slightest membrane of light and time. These flickering
> moments are the beginning, and end, of everything.

The next day, while walking in the woods, these lines return to
me, as does my entire dream, when I suddenly understand that they
are a last prayer to my beloved teacher, Cleo. I am tramping along
the river and looking up at a heron's nest in an enormous sycamore
tree, when my senses grow oddly acute. Beyond the creaking sway of
that tree and the dry rasp of each of its leaves in the wind, I feel her
presence. And I *know:* The fear of night was the fear of death, of
separation. The words my heart was making while I slept were
searching for Cleo's eye and ear, for one last reading.

Creatures

There are a thousand ways for a mouse to enter the henhouse. It's a sieve. They scuttle inside at first frost. In *Leaves of Grass*, Walt Whitman claims: "A mouse is miracle enough to stagger sextillions of infidels."[18] But a mouse is also miracle enough to *become* sextillions of infidels: two turn into ten, and then ten into fifty, all within a month or two. I like them, but it gets crowded. Last week, I woke to find two sitting on the workbench in a pool of moonlight, noisily munching on opposite sides of a large, red Cortland apple. Each had chewed away a tablespoon or so of the flesh and left a tiny pile of apple skin gnawings. The next morning, I bought cheap wooden traps, smeared them with chunky peanut butter, and set them on the trails of excrement the mice left along the floor. I cringed at the two neck-cracking snaps that night, but it seemed necessary rather than cruel.

A few days later, I agonized over a fleeing mouse that somehow jumped a foot off the ground into the crack between the hinged side of the door and the jam, just as I was leaving. I nearly cut him in two.

Grossly pinched in the crack, his bulging black eyes pleaded with me, but it was too late. I closed the door to free him and he fell bloody and mangled to the ground. I killed him quickly with a brick, but felt his desperate gaze all day.

I usually only see mice inside at night, but today one was lured out in the middle of the afternoon by a trap someone else had set. He carefully nibbled all the peanut butter off the metal bait plate, and then walked right over the trap, setting it off on his head. Ten minutes later a second mouse appeared and began nosing the trap with the dead mouse all over the floor, and nibbling at the metal bars, as if trying to free him. Was this the "spouse mouse" coming to grieve its loss? I felt awful. I kept watching. When he finally flipped the trap over, his motivation was clear. He was after a bit of peanut butter on the wooden base of the trap, under the dead mouse's belly. He was trying to move the dead mouse out of the way so he could get to the food.

Perhaps I have read *Stuart Little* to my children too many times. I wanted to believe that the desire to love triumphs over the instinct to survive—even in mice. I wanted to believe that we are related.

We are. A recent study of the mouse's genome revealed that both mice and humans have about 30,000 genes, with only about 300 unique to either species. Human beings share 99 percent of their genes with mice—including the genes required to make a tail![19] Yet that single percentage point is immense. It is why people refer to other people as "animals" only when they wish to insult them. *Animals* don't love; they reproduce. They don't reflect; they respond. They are instinctive, irrational, violent.

Humans, however, have reason—that beautiful and confusing gift. Like truth, reason is subjective and relative. It leads to good and evil: to the theory of relativity, the polio vaccine, the civil rights movement; but also to slavery, Auschwitz, poisoned rivers, holes in the ozone. If not coupled with compassion, human reason is no less cruel and no more just than animal instinct.

Does reason enhance the human capacity to attend to the world? Our five senses are less complex and useful than in other mammals. We cannot follow our nose or ears through the woods to our children or to food. I sometimes wonder if this limited awareness reinforces our carefully reasoned exploitation of the natural world, if our minimal ability to taste and hear and see that world prevents us from rejoining it. Has reason itself, that rare ability to judge and discern, disconnected us?

I watch out my window as a chipmunk chews up a mulberry and packs the little bits in his bulging cheeks. And I wonder: How did the human, the reason-able species, develop the power to destroy all others? Why can we not resist the temptation to commodify and sell the world, rather than simply belong to it? What went wrong?

Somewhere between learning to walk and a B.A. degree we forget that we are animals: connected and created. Creatures. We cannot manufacture ourselves (or at least not yet). Like mice and raccoons we are squeezed from the warm cavity of our mothers, born alive and squirming. Later we die. Out hearts fail, and our nerves stop firing. If we were not embalmed and placed in a sealed airless coffin, we, too, would rot in a ditch like road kill. We would belong again.

This afternoon I witnessed the death of another small creature. Unlike the mouse I caught in the door, this death seemed holy rather than tragic. While pumping my bike along Flynn Road, the two-lane blacktop that runs by the farm, I noticed a glint of yellow on the road ahead. I coasted up near the ditch to find a goldfinch lying in the gravel. The feathers were bright and clean—no evidence it had hit a windshield or been raked by a crow—a perfect specimen. Yet it was not flapping or trying to escape, and its eyes were closed. It lay in the gravel softly breathing. I got closer, put my face down near its feathers, hoping to find out what was wrong. And then this: Its eyes opened— two shiny black beads peering at me for several seconds. I felt it sensed that I was there and had used all its energy to confirm its suspicion, to see what I was. Then the eyes closed, the breathing slowed, and stopped. The goldfinch died, and I had no idea why—disease, poison, or, hopefully, a natural end. Perhaps he had waited too long to head south.

I'm still wondering about that open-eyed instant of connection, about being the last living thing the bird saw. Does dying alone matter to creatures that live by instinct rather than reason? Maybe the goldfinch didn't even notice me in its last moment, but was looking beyond—at the empty sky, the rustling weeds, the stark silhouette of a maple tree—sensing, not aloneness, but belonging.

WINTER

Death is not the end of everything, because we are not everything.

—Dorothee Soelle[1]

Presence

We are most deeply asleep at the switch when we fancy we control any switches at all. We sleep to time's hurdy-gurdy; we wake, if we ever wake, to the silence of God.

—ANNIE DILLARD[2]

I rarely come here in the winter, particularly now, in January. The short, bitter days make it hard to leave Carol and the kids. Though we don't huddle together in a tree hollow or turn our metabolisms down to "barely alive," the cold does slow us down. We read more, even play chess or board games. On the coldest nights we make a fire and tell stories and watch the logs burn. Sometimes I watch the kids watching the fire and catch them in a moment when they are utterly lost in the flames. I follow their eyes, seeking what they seek. Whatever it is that we find in the glowing smolder is what makes me want to stay put, to burrow in.

Another problem with winter in the henhouse: no heat. By Halloween, even with heavy plastic stapled over all the windows and a portable 1000–watt electric heater (think large toaster oven) blasting my feet, it's too cold. My fingers numb up. So now, on one of those rare winter weekends, I work and sleep in the farmhouse, which is just fifty yards from the henhouse. It's cold, too, but a wood-burning stove heats the living room and the large adjacent kitchen.

I have three days to write. They move slowly. My words follow the sun. I wake at dawn and write until dusk. When things go best I *lose* time—can no longer assign numbers to given points of the day. I become the day, belong to it. But when the words don't come, the isolation begins to nag, and I long for the comforting face of a clock.

The last breath of sunlight diffuses into the dry air. I fill the bird feeder and take a long walk in the darkening woods. Later, I fry three eggs for dinner, eat them by the wood stove, call Carol and the kids, write a letter to a friend, and then go upstairs to bed. The second floor is a bunk house, an open room with five beds, a large table, and three (un)easy chairs. I crawl under two old sleeping bags with my clothes on, including a sweater, and then—as an afterthought—decide to remove my stocking cap. I reach over to flip on the gooseneck reading lamp and pull the sleeping bag back up to my neck.

I'm reading *Technopoly*, Neil Postman's take on the detriments of modern technology. He includes a history of the clock. The first ones had a religious origin. Twelfth-century Benedictine monks needed a way to reliably mark their seven daily prayer sessions. The mechanical clock was invented to tell the monks when to ring the bell to call the community to prayer at the appointed times. By the middle of the fourteenth century the lure of such a clock, of measured time, spread outside the monastery walls to the world of commerce, introducing "the idea of regular production, regular working hours and a standardized project." Postman doesn't miss the irony: "…the clock was invented by men who wanted to devote themselves more rigorously to God; it ended as the technology of greatest use to men who wished to devote themselves to the accumulation of money. In the eternal struggle between God and mammon the clock quite unpredictably favored the latter."[3]

A little hungry and a little cold, I can't sleep. I lie there wondering about God's time, and thinking about our children, who inherently understand this *presence* better than I do. I pull out a couple of my old spiral journals, and read. The first entry is more recent:

> This morning Tessa and Abby were huddled in their underwear on the kitchen linoleum eating cereal out of green plastic parfait glasses. They draped a large yellow silk shawl

over their heads; it covered them both down to their waists. When they heard my steps, they stopped crunching and grew quiet. Then they erupted in giggling. "Shsh, Abby," Tessa said. "I think it's a bear." I knew what they wanted—for me to growl like I sometimes do and then chase them into the closet. But in my rush to get to work I ignored their invitation. "O.K. girls, it's 7:30—time to get dressed and sit down for breakfast," I said. They kept waiting. "Come on Daddy, you're supposed to be the bear," Tessa said. "Yah, Dahdee," Abby chimed in. "You 'posed to be duh bear." But in my distraction I couldn't come into the moment, couldn't BE the bear.

Today Tessa was watching a cartoon while I cleaned the kitchen. During the program one of the characters announced, "I'm bored." Tessa then repeated the phrase every hour or so for the rest of the afternoon, not knowing for sure what it meant. Having no idea how to define "boredom" for a three year old, I felt frustrated. I wanted to say it is laziness, or the opposite of paying attention, or the opposite of response-ability. I wanted to quote Walt Whitman: "Boredom is simply the emotional underside of insensitivity." Or Tolstoy: "Boredom is the desire for desires." But finally, I said that a bored person is probably a bit sad and a bit tired.

"Are you ever sad, Daddy?"

"Yes," I say.

"Are you ever tired?" she asks.

"Yeah, I get worn out sometimes."

Then I asked her if she wanted to go in the kitchen and get her watercolors out. She did. She pulled out her art box, fished out the long, plastic yellow case, snapped it open, and dribbled in a little water. The oval cakes of pigment softened into puddles of color. She tore off one piece of paper from her tablet for me, and one for her. I put on some water for tea and opened all the windows. Soon a humming mower, a twittering wren on the electric line, the rubber thump of a basketball on concrete, the smell of cut grass, and my own childhood came drifting in through the screens. We rubbed and swished our brushes in the raw greens and reds and blues and made great timeless swirls leading nowhere.

I fall asleep dreaming of those colors, with the reading light and my glasses still on. The next day the thermometer on the end table by my bed reads 39 degrees, just 25 degrees warmer than outside. The sun is up but still low, backlighting the white pines in the distance. I crawl out of my cocoon, stumble downstairs, start the fire in the stove, and set up a card table 3 feet in front of it. A slow stream of smoke follows the draw of the flue, out into the cold. Then the orange flames grow and grow in the cast-iron chamber until they become the flickering hands of the clock of God—not pointing at anything, but dancing with abandon. Wood burns to ash, which I will scatter in the garden, which will turn into loam, which will feed the tomatoes and green beans, which will feed us, and on and on. Ashes to ashes.

God's time is rooted not in limitation or division but *relationship*. Even numerical time is relational, and less exact than we imagine. A "minute" is derived from the Babylonian fractional system and Ptolemy's division of the circle into sixty sections. Yet in daily life a minute can seem arbitrary. As a toddler Abby once flew into a rage because she wanted me to get her a book while I was emptying the dishwasher. "Just a minute, " I said. The second time I said this, she went ballistic. But I couldn't understand what she was screaming back at me. Tessa translated: "She's saying, '*How long is a minute?*'"

Tessa already knew that a "minute" was not a fixed increment, but contextual. She had also given up loudly counting to sixty, which used to calm her while she waited. Now she too uses the word as a transition rather than a statement of fact. She also just learned the second pronunciation and meaning of "minute." We were trying to decide how they are related. They share the same Latin root, *minutus* (small). One word is a noun and supposedly exact (i.e., sixty seconds) and the other is an adjective and more general. Even so, both words attempt to measure something and fail beautifully. What they measure is relationship. A red ant is not minute, but *immense,* in contrast to a mitochondria. A minute is how long it takes to do something.

My theory of relativity: Rigidly *controlled* time lends the illusion of precision, while intensely *creative* time reveals that it cannot be controlled. Perhaps we control time in the search for measurement, but create time in the search for meaning.

The coldness of the farmhouse kitchen reminds me how alone I am. I make a pot of coffee. The rhythmic dripping and warm bitter smell comfort me. I turn on the radio and listen to the news. The President is proclaiming the virtues of his war. He says the same words over and over: "terror," "evil," and "freedom." He says "the future of our children is at stake." I've heard this rhetoric for most of my life, but it is more painful now, as a parent. I'm thinking of the thousands of Iraqi children and their parents who we incinerated rather than liberated—of how we destroyed homes and the water supply and the food stocks all in the "march toward freedom." Then, for a moment, I try to imagine the people who actually live there: the horror of one family, the timelessness of the nightmare we have unleashed, the burning of flesh and breaking of bones.

Last month, I spent a night with Tessa in the hospital. She had to stay for several days because she had the stomach flu and became dehydrated. Confused and exhausted, she spent all night retching and heaving, until 5 a.m., when she finally collapsed into sleep. During those late hours I rubbed her back and reassured her over and over again that she would soon heal, that things would get better. And they did. But what I'm wondering now is what an Iraqi parent will tell his child, if there is no bed, no IV, no medicine, no water—if the present is desperate, and the future worse. How will they muster any hope?

I have no answers. I pull out my most recent journal entry. It was scribbled on a folded piece of lined notebook paper and stapled in.

Today I took Abby and Bennett to a big rally in Chicago against the war in Iraq. Carol is staying with Tessa, who has been sick in the hospital for the past few days. She's got the flu and is dehydrated.

When we arrived in the Loop it was seven degrees, much colder with the wind—so cold that Abby was crying. She has been to many such rallies, and is of course always more interested in the snack options and whether her friends will be there than the purpose of the rally. I wrapped my scarf around her face so only her eyes peeked through and carried her for a while, while pushing the stroller. But she kept crying and remained unusually sad. I wrapped Bennett tightly in a quilt. But coming to the rally was beginning to seem like a bad idea.

After walking a few more long blocks, we reached the crowd and nestled in among the thousand or so bodies, out of the wind. Abby tried hard to rise to the occasion. We marched and chanted for 45 minutes—until our feet and hands were numb and we had all had enough. As we made our way back to the parking lot against a brutal wind, Abby finally looked up at me and said, "I hope Tessa's OK." She was on the verge of tears. "Me too," I said, only then realizing that Tessa, not the cold, was the source of her sadness.

I sit staring out the front window at Flynn Road, thankful for this wrinkled scrap of love. I think about war and children, and about Abby's simple moment of compassion. What was she teaching me? That the smallest acts of love also heal the world's suffering? I don't think Abby could imagine a war, or the thousands of innocent parents and children our military has bombed. But she could imagine her sister.

Making Time

Life is short. So move very slowly.

—THAI SAYING

D awn. Light seeps into the cold stone farmhouse wherever it can. I start the fire, turn on the computer and a classic FM radio station. A lonely oboe plays a Vivaldi concerto. This afternoon, after three days of work, I will return home to Chicago. Thinking more about my family than my writing, I pull out my seeds file to try to regain focus…and find a photo. Pictures often help jumpstart my writing. I like how they frame time but don't stop it, how the viewer must overlay the present tense of the photo with his own, how this paradox can catalyze memory.

The decade-old photo is of Carol when we were teaching in the Philippines. She's surrounded by her theology students. She's hot and tired and pregnant with Tessa, our first child. It was challenging: the dripping heat, no electricity during the day, very few books or resources. Yet in the photo Carol's eyes seem calm and thankful.

As the only North Americans in the village where we lived, we prompted a lot of *tsismis* (gossip), particularly around one issue: children. Our Filipino friends were in dismay: married eight years and still childless? Figuring it was my problem, some of my students insisted I eat *balut* (boiled duck embryos) to make myself more virile. I tried to eat them but couldn't keep them down. We always feigned ignorance when questions about starting a family were raised, not wanting to explain (again) that our waiting was intentional.

When Carol became pregnant, we sensed both joy and relief among our Filipino colleagues. One woman said that she was glad that they had "helped us," that our baby was "made in the Philippines." Students and colleagues greeted Carol with eyes that recognized her pregnancy as miracle. Women would gently place their hands on the bulging curve of her belly, listening with their fingertips, and then hug her in celebration. If Carol was nauseous, or worn down by the humidity, the dean encouraged her to go home. And it didn't seem to be just because she was a foreigner.

The Ilocos region of the Philippines is, of course, very different from Chicago. It is a lower-tech culture that perceives time differently. People had no social security or health insurance and few basic conveniences, like telephones and cars. At the time, neither did they have pagers, voice mail, cell phones, or e-mail. So it was impossible to be more than one place at a time. The extended family was more intact and offered more possibilities for childcare. The "it takes a village" idea was a way of life rather than political rhetoric.

The last few months of Carol's pregnancy were stateside. When we returned to the U.S., our friends were excited; but they followed their congratulations with a familiar question: "What are you going to do about work?" Even a well-timed pregnancy represented both miracle and dilemma, both gift and burden, in U.S. culture.

Now, a decade later, we have three of those miraculous dilemmas prancing around our house in their PJs. Like many, we are trying to figure out how to balance work and parenthood, to make time to be a family. The desperate nature of this problem is captured by the title of a recent book: *365 Ways to Save Time with Kids*. The idiocy of this idea prompted me to conjure a more honest title: "How to Accelerate Your Kids' Lives and Spend Less Time with Them Every Single Day." The book points to a central contradiction: What we usually mean when we say "save time" in our culture is "get more stuff done."

Were I to believe the media, the key to achieving a well-nurtured family and meaningful work identities for both parents is time management, and the key to successful time management is technology. A TV commercial a few years ago depicted a father who was simultaneously working on an oil rig in the middle of the ocean somewhere and, on a cell phone, talking his wife through the birth of their child. The miracle of technology enabled the father to "not miss" their baby's birth, to "be" there.

Why does our culture aspire to this kind of being? Cell phones, those chirpy icons of connectedness, sometimes seem less a source of happiness than a balm against loneliness. Everywhere I look at my college, I see people checking and rechecking their cell phones as if their lives depended on it, as if the pulsing fist of plastic was a vital organ. Why do some so fear turning them off? What do they think they will miss? Perhaps the connection they most desire is really a human one—the tilted smile, the forgiving eyes, a warm, heavy arm around a shoulder—a connection where touch is real.

Kairos and Chronos

The births of our children taught me how inherently unmanageable meaningful time can be. But my birth memories are not in conventional time—not in what the Greeks called *chronos* (a measurable point in time), but in what they called *kairos* (the fullness of time). Birth is "kairotic": an immeasurable, uncontrollable moment that has never before occurred and will never occur again. Each of our children's births was a moment of unparalleled opportunity for meaning, for beauty, a quintessentially present moment that initiated both the being of our children and of ourselves as parents. And to me as an observer/supporter, birth seemed a moment of simultaneous physical separation and spiritual reconnection between mother and child, a creative rather than productive moment.

But in the past few years, as the girls have started school and fallen into their own schedules, I have lost much of the *kairos* sense of time that birth teaches. I sometimes see our kids as paradoxical anchors that are forever tied to my life. They provide spiritual and moral stability, faithfully holding on to me through the stormiest of seas, teaching me how to live a five-sensed life, refusing to cut me loose despite my flaws. But during my selfish moments, they seem like a heavy weight that prevents me from moving toward the fulfillment of personal goals. On these hectic, overscheduled days I feel an intense desire to get control of our frenetic lives. But when I yield to the delusion of time management, multi-tasking leads to multi-being, to emotional and intellectual fragmentation.

I'm beginning to understand that while I can't "make time" for my children, they can sometimes make it for me. When I watch and listen carefully, they teach me how to slow down enough to discern the limits of an autopiloted life. When Tessa and Abby and Bennett kneel wide-eyed on the sidewalk over an anthill, or chase lightening bugs in the cool lull between dusk and dark, or quietly monitor a robin sitting on its eggs in the crook of an elm tree, they are making time for me. When they create mini-dramas with their stuffed animals and plastic dolls in a world they construct from shoeboxes, sofa cushions, and small blocks of wood, they are making time for me.

Children ask, and remind us to ask, what our hands are for. They finger paint. They squeeze cold oatmeal between their fingers at breakfast. They rub marinara sauce in their hair and eyebrows at dinner and don't care if it dries into cement. They know parents can be bread makers as well as breadwinners. They remind us that the linger of yeast and the warm quiet dough rising on the kitchen table is not a romanticized image from a bygone era, but represents one of a thousand choices that parents perpetually make between time and money.

Because they have not yet unlearned the wonders of their senses, nor the sacred efficiency of the natural world, children can teach us how to re-member lives that are rooted in connectedness, in relationship. As parents who were once children, we can easily recount how differently time evolved when we were little, the literal *sense of time*—how our fingers, tongue, nose, eyes, and ears perceived the world—that physical curiosity that led us to questions we can still live in. When children make time for us, they also make time for God, a time of *kairos*.

"Jesus kept on telling us we should try to be more like children," reflected Dorothy Day in her seventies:

> Be more open to life, curious about it, trusting of it; and be less cynical and skeptical and full of ourselves, as we so often are when we get older. I'm not romanticizing childhood, no. I can recall my "bad" behavior…But I also remember all the

wondering I did, all the questions I had about life and God
and the purpose of things. And even now, when I'm praying
or trying to keep my spiritual side going, before I know it,
I'm a little girl.[4]

I clean up the farmhouse, pack the car, and head off down Flynn
Road. Cruising toward the hazy red horizon, I take a deep breath.
Soon I, too, am a little boy again—dreaming of our family vacations
here in Michigan: crawling on my knees through the weeds with a
dented coffee can, coaxing crickets and grasshoppers to jump inside.
Then I'm lying on my back in the pine needles, watching the swaying
patterns of tree and sky and cloud far above me. Then I'm bobbing in
Lake Michigan with my three older brothers. We are all treading
water and riding the waves on a stormy day. I'm listening to their
stories and the magic of their laughter…

When the dreams end, I look around and see I'm in Gary, Indiana.
How did I get here so quickly? As I thread my way through a traffic
jam at five miles per hour, I open my window to the smell and taste
of Gary Steel's smelting pots. Then traffic stops. This is the kind of
waiting I can't take. I see an exit I want, and the ramp is empty; but
I can't get through the other four lanes of cars in time. The world
again tightens around me. I stop wondering and start worrying about
all the things I never seem to get done, about finding and making
and losing time.

The Nature of Violence

In violence we forget who we are.
—MARY McCarthy[5]

It has been several weeks since my last visit to the farm. I returned last night. It was nearly midnight when I pulled onto Flynn Road. About 100 yards from the farmhouse my headlights caught the outline of a furry animal with large triangular ears and a long tail crawling on top of some other animal. The blacktop was dark and silent, so I threw the car in reverse and whirred backward until I could train my headlights on the bloody pointed mouth of a possum feeding on fresh road kill—a raccoon.

A mid-February cold snap had ended abruptly. In the past twenty-four hours the temperature climbed from 11 to 46 degrees. Possums and raccoons don't hibernate; they are "winter sleepers"—meaning that after holing up in some tree trunk during the recent bitter weather, these animals were lured from lethargy by the "heat wave," and their stomachs.

Perhaps I'm a voyeur, parking six feet away from the possum—with my lights still on and my window down. Ravenously hungry, he ignored me. He peeled three long strips of fur back over the raccoon's rib cage like he was shucking an ear of corn, then plunged his face into the opening, under the roof of bones and into the steaming organs. The immense sparkling bowl of the night sky seemed to magnify rather than absorb the sound of the tearing flesh and of the possum's eerie breathing. Then he clamped onto the stomach and began backing up until the gut snapped. When it did, he was almost under the car. I could have reached down and touched him. I stuck my head out the window for a better look; and he whirled, gave a ceremonious hiss, and showed me his teeth—about fifty, short and jagged. Then he went right back to work. Clearly, I was an inconvenience, not a threat.

After he had chomped through the aorta, I was startled by how easily I recognized the raccoon's heart. The possum snatched out the dripping lump of muscle and crunched it up like a large apricot that had not yet ripened into softness, into its sweet summer tang. At that moment the beam of light on the bloody mangle made me feel like I was watching a scene from a war rather than the cycle of creation. It seemed an act of appalling violence. But in providing for itself and thus its offspring, the possum was also maintaining the balance of things, the network of relationships that sustain the cycle of nature.

At the college where I teach, my students and I have been struggling to better understand the complex problem of violence for the past few years. In a research course, we first read an essay by philosopher John Modschiedler called "Understanding Violence." Relying heavily on etymology, he defines violence this way.

> It is a ripping apart, a tearing out (of context), the end product of not thinking of things in relationship. Violence is a scattering. Scattering is the opposite of gathered togetherness— community. Violence is an assault on community, on belongingness, on relationship...[6]

We spent the rest of the semester reading books and articles that apply this idea to the violence in our lives—to how domestic violence and racism and poverty and militarism and the war on the environment all rip apart the dream of "gathered togetherness," of real community.

This week at the farm, however, my only text is the natural world. And the damp muddy story of this late winter thaw tells me that the possum's heart-ripping meal was not an act of violence, but its antithesis—as is the act of the coyote pouncing on a cottontail that wanders too far from its nest or the robins who will soon return to start wildly yanking worms from the mud. Prey and predator both belong because they live and die in a balanced cycle of relationship.

But consider the relationship between the human and the rest of the natural world. The human drives the car that kills the raccoon that "got in its way." He leaves it there—doesn't skin it or eat it or even pull the carcass off the asphalt to rot in the ditch. The possum compensates. So do a couple of starlings the next day, when they raucously peck out the raccoon's eyes, the only soft tissue they can find. At dusk a cat wanders by and drags the raccoon off the road and into the ditch by the matted stump of its tail. But then it loses interest. Two days later the temperature warms up to 70 degrees, and a platoon of ants joins the beetles and mites and bacteria that have begun to eat and digest the carcass back into the earth. This is not violence, but the stewardship of instinct.

The animal most adept at breaking the balance of nature lives not by instinct, but by reason. Intensely self-conscious, and with unparalleled intellect and language skills, only humans can conceive of their "role" in nature, a role we increasingly view as material opportunity rather than moral responsibility. Being human is less about belonging to creation than controlling it. And this ignorance is the source of much violence to our own species and to the whole of the biosphere.

Seminary taught me that religion could help reduce or resolve the problem of human violence. The Latin root of the word *religion* means "to bind together." This implies a social ethic and thus a remedy to the core disrelation and "ripping apart." But while many religious leaders and communities have modeled alternatives to violence, religion also has catalyzed and/or validated much violent behavior, including most wars. Perhaps the problem is the alternative meaning of "to bind." To bind also means to enslave. "Religious" Euro-Americans enslaved Africans and sold them at auctions like cattle. The U.S. government limited the human species to the light-skinned, defining a "Negro" as 3/5 of a human being. And our military killed hundreds of thousands of Native Americans ("savages") in the quest for more land.

This tradition of "the enemy as animal," and thus expendable, continues. In the 60s the North Vietnamese, when not referred to as gooks or dinks, were called "Indians" by the U.S. military. In the '90s, U.S. pilots called the bombing of retreating Iraqis "a turkey shoot." A former student who was in Iraq last year said he heard fellow soldiers refer to Arabs as "sand niggers." Violence against those defined as "subhuman" has been historically legitimized and widely accepted in this country.

This mindset is consistent with our attitude toward the billions of nonhuman creatures with which we share the earth—the bullfrogs and salmon, the oak trees and meadowlarks. The war on the environment is also fierce. We continue to "rip apart" nonhuman communities and cultures, to assault the "gathered togetherness" of the earth entire. I have sometimes heard Christians use a Genesis-based argument for "man's dominion" over creation to justify their "right" to develop (destroy), market, and sell every square foot of it. This view of the natural world as a war for domination, rather than a web of interdependency, has become governmental policy. But there are other models. The possum, too, has its wisdom.

Mitakuye Oyas'in

This afternoon, in between the pages of my dictionary, I find a sprig of sage I picked in the meadow last fall. I crush it with my thumb and fingers and hold it to my nose and think of the Lakota people—how they sometimes burn dried sage when they pray, how the curl of smoke rising and diffusing in the air is a metaphor for their prayer going into the world.

The Lakota of the Great Plains have spent the past three centuries adapting to and recovering from the violence of Euro-American "development." They understand "the assault on community" and "scattering" that Modschiedler alludes to. And some are still trying to offer an alternative to the "dominion" worldview, to find a way to approach the world as community rather than commodity.

I learned about some of these alternatives over the past decade or so—through numerous visits to several Lakota reservations in South Dakota. I don't want to romanticize these experiences or slip into a kind of imperialist nostalgia. These reservations are violent in their own way. They are the poorest rural regions in the United States.

Alcoholism and unemployment rage. Health care is poor. Despair is the result of a history of scattering, of the ripping apart of this culture. But also present is a resilient spiritual tradition rooted in the natural balance of things.

The Lakota language has no word for religion. The ideas of "church" and "worship" are not separated from the natural world, but a part of it. And humans, too, are a part of creation, not above it. This equality is apparent everywhere. For example, the Lakota classify animals by how they move: the four-legged (raccoons), the winged (birds), the two-legged (people), the creepers (bugs) and the swimmers (fish). A traditional Lakota may pray for a deer he has killed or for medicinal plants he has gathered in thanksgiving, because he knows he depends on them and the rest of creation for sustenance, for survival.

When participating in Lakota ceremonies, one of the most common phrases spoken is *mitakuye oyas'in*, which means "all my relatives" or "I am related to all that is." When a person enters or exits a ceremony or finishes speaking, he typically says "mitakuye oyas'in." This simple prayer of relatedness is central to Lakota tradition, and I am always struck by how the idea is not discussed, but lived. Mitakuye oyas'in is not a theory but a physical experience, a reenactment of nature's relatedness. The *inipi*, or sweat bath ceremony, provides a good example of this. The ceremony includes the elements of creation: fire, water, air, and earth. The lodge symbolizes creation: It is circular, unending—like a bird's nest, or a tepee, or the sky or the earth, or the cycle of the seasons.

Oddly, my first sweat is the one I remember the most viscerally. Many years ago I participated in a seminary "field study" course. We focused on the paradoxical relationship between Lakota culture and Christianity.[7]

Darkness had fallen by the time we arrived at our host's home. We walked down a long rocky hill to the sweat lodge near a creek. The structure was lower and wider than I imagined. The roof peaked at four feet and was made of large canvas tarps and carpet remnants thrown over a red willow frame. Opposite the lodge entrance (a flap of canvas) blazed a large, hot fire in which the rocks were being prepared. We stood and listened to Martin, the Lakota elder who would lead us. As he added wood to the fire, he told us that the rocks, which were iridescent with heat, were the center of the earth and that soon we would sit around them and pray.

When the rocks were ready, we all undressed. It was dark by then, and cold—15 or 20 degrees—and windy, with a thick blanket of snow on the ground. As we stood there shivering in our gym shorts, Martin told us that those who enter the sweat lodge become children again as they crawl naked on hands and knees back into the warm, wet womb of their Mother.

I didn't really understand this until I got down on all fours and crawled in. As instructed, we said "*mitakuye oyas'in*" upon entering, the same thing we would say after each prayer and when we exited. The dirt floor was hard and damp. Martin was already in, sitting on the other side. All eight of us crawled toward him, filling in the circle. We crouched tightly together in the heavy darkness around the empty fire pit—the center of the center. Someone outside lifted a grapefruit-sized white-hot rock from the fire with a pitchfork, threaded it through the open-flap door hole, and dropped it in the pit. The next three rocks were a little bigger and seemed to double the temperature in the lodge. Martin arranged them into the four directions with a deer antler, sprinkled sweet grass and cedar shavings on them, and prayed.

When twelve smoking rocks were all arranged—a foot or less from our bare toes—whoever was tending the fire outside closed the flap. The lodge was hot and black, and the holy glowing rocks both beautiful and frightening. By then we were all dripping on each other. I could feel the fear rising in the circle. I have done many sweats since that one, but I'm still always a little afraid of the confinement, and of being burnt or unable to breathe. Letting go of the fear, sharing the suffering, and trusting the leader is how one belongs to the circle. But the ceremony is not about machismo. If at any time the lodge grows too hot to bear, one simply says "*mitakuye oyas'in*" and scoots out.

Martin sloshed the dipper in the metal bucket. He sang as he ladled water on the rocks. In the commingling of light and darkness the rocks cried out; their arms of steam lifted heavy waves of heat that pulled us all together into their prayer. I cannot say more about the specifics of the ceremony, other than this: Time disappears in the *inipi*. Or maybe there is only time, a time of unfolding relationship: between water and flesh, plant and animal, self and world. Was it an hour or two hours later when we crawled out of the steaming womb slick as newborns? *"Mitakuye oyas'in"* we each said as we met the startling rush of cold air and tried to stand on wobbly legs.

That night on the frozen cusp of the South Dakota plain, I stood under a dome of flickering stars and watched the soft fingers of moonlight reaching for the barren trees, for the mirror of the frozen creek, and for us. And I wondered if I had ever felt so small, or like I knew so little, or so deeply connected to the whole.

By dusk cold has descended, and a heavy snow is falling. A male cardinal pauses on a low branch to scan the ground for seed, then drops into flight, flaps out of my frame of vision. The dipping flash of red is the only bright color I've seen all day against the washed-out grays and browns of weeds and barren trees. Other birds fill the trees, juncos and sparrows, but I can barely distinguish them from the limbs they perch on. Then I see a crow walking on a dark mound in the yard. I look closer: the road kill raccoon. The crow has either found a bit of loose meat or is starving, because he is wildly pecking at the carcass.

As I watch the crow digging in the wad of fur and bones, and the snow floating down and coating the trees that line Flynn Road, I'm filled with sadness. It is now, at the end of the day, when I listen to a bit of news on the radio and leaf through the *Chicago Tribune*. I hear the stories and see the pictures of the war: the grisly dead in Iraq, the singed flesh and hovering flies. I become angry again and want answers. I want the President and the Congress to show their "moral courage" on the battlefield, like many of my own students have. I want the mothers of the dead soldiers to be the military strategists. I want Iraqi civilian deaths to matter in *this* country. I want to ban revenge and preemption as foreign policy. I want to know how to choose life again…

But I don't know how, and my rants are hollow. I am alone. All I have is the silent rhythm of the snow—the snow that falls on the boots of soldiers and the bare feet of mothers, on smiling children and bombed out hospitals. Here it falls on the hungry crow and on the shivering sparrows. It falls on the raccoons that make it across the road at night, and on those that don't. It falls on the farmhouse and on these quiet gravel roads. It falls and falls and falls.

Tonight I'll dream of its surrender to the sun, of the melting, and how it will soak the tulip bulbs and the day lilies and the black-eyed Susans and all the other tentacles of root twisting beneath the woods in their slow cycle of resurrection.

Perfectly Flawed

*Except in idea, perfection is as wild as light; there is
no hand laid on it.*

—Wendell Berry[8]

February in Chicago is a gray slushy crawl toward spring. It keeps
me in winter mode—more in my head than my hands and feet,
and still reliant on books and the fireplace to distract me from the
cold, short days. Today, after school, Tessa and I got all bundled up
and walked to the library to browse. She found a new book by Lois
Lowry, a favorite author. I found Anne Lamott's three memoirs on a
display shelf and noticed they concern the same three strands of life
I'm writing about—family, faith, and writing. How convenient!
Operating Instructions (1993) explores the process of becoming a
parent; *Bird by Bird* (1994) explores the process of becoming a writer;
and *Traveling Mercies* (1999) explores the process of faith. Collectively,
the books pose the question I'm living in: What does learning how to
believe in God have to do with learning how to parent and learning
how to write? Can these three arts somehow be woven into an
integrated life? I checked out the books and mulled them over for a
few weeks.

After a while the themes began to blur. *Operating Instructions*, a diary of her son's first year of life, is also about faith: "How did some fabulously cerebral and black-humored cynic like myself come to fall for that Christian lunacy to see the cross not as an end, but a beginning…my faith is a great mystery. It has me shaking my head."[9] Lamott then quotes a line someone scribbled underneath an ancient crucifix in a nearby church: "Jesus has no arms but ours to do his work and to show his love." She concludes, "…these are the only operating instructions I will ever need."[10]

The book then doesn't "instruct" how to treat a breast-duct infection or insert an anal thermometer. It does ask you to live out your doubts and fears with a writer who is less concerned with how to parent than how to *believe:* in a tiny, completely dependent baby; in a lonely, imperfect self; in an elusive God; and in the possibility of a transforming community. Faith and community seem even more necessary to Lamott because the major characters are exceedingly vulnerable: herself, a single mother who is a recovering alcoholic and bulimic; Sam, her newborn baby; and her best friend Pammy, who is dying from breast cancer. In the end, however, the interweaving of their lives prompts joy rather than sympathy. They co-construct an ethic that sustains them: *vulnerability is not weakness, but the heart of a shared humanity.*

From her loneliness Lamott struggles to reach out for help when she needs it, to become dependent on others, to find a community. In *Operating Instructions* she writes: "I'm learning to call people all the time to ask for help, which is about the hardest thing I can think of doing. I'm always suggesting that other people do it, but it really is awful…I tell my writing students to get in the habit of calling one another, because writing is such a scary, lonely business…It turns out mothering is the same way."[11]

This is a shared theme among all three books: We can't do it alone. The arts of faith, parenting, and writing usually require a supportive community to sustain one's self-confidence and personal integrity.

Another of her mantras is, "Take it one day at a time." Every day write a page. Every day listen for God. Every day listen to your child. Eventually you will arrive where you need to be. One of her rationales for this approach is suggested in a kind of lament she aims at God toward the end of *Traveling Mercies.* "God: I wish you could have some permanence, a guarantee or two, the unconditional love we all long for…I never get an answer…In the meantime I have learned that all we have is the moment and the imperfect love of people."[12]

The only kind of love is imperfect love.

I think of this now as I watch Tessa and Abby cutting out hearts for Valentines Day. They fold, cut, reopen, and then paste the little red-and-white shapes on cards for their classmates. The hearts are symmetrical: two inverted tear drops merged exactly at the middle, forming a perfect valley at the top. They bear little resemblance to the human heart—that fist-sized, asymmetrical knot of muscles with the tubes coming out.

When we walk along Lake Michigan together, we like to look for heart rocks. They are not symmetrical either. Most are oval or quasi-triangles with a little dip somewhere barely indicating the "top." Sometimes only the person who finds the rock can recognize the shape and has to explain how they see the heart. Someone could probably find the heart in any rock lying along the shore. They are like people: all different, imperfect, and beautiful.

I like how Lamott explores this idea—the delusions of perfection—particularly for artists: "[G]o ahead and make big scrawls and mistakes," she advises. "Perfection is a mean, frozen form of idealism, while messes are the artist's true friend. What people somehow forgot to mention when we were children is that we need to make messes to find out who we are and why we are here."[13]

Art is a process of discovering who you are and why you're here.

I look around my basement "office": four stained coffee cups, stacks of letters and file folders and sketch pads scattered everywhere, a half-eaten bag of red licorice, two beer bottles, a fistful of crumpled receipts, and some splattered watercolor palettes. Amid the clutter is one of Tessa's old crayon drawings—a brown rectangle desk and behind it a smiling round-headed peach-colored man with a beard—me. She wrote "Mr. Mongomre-Fat, Techer" on top and then taped it on the door. Her lovely drawing and my mess make me wonder about Lamott's advice, about whether the "big scrawls and mistakes" I make as an adult differ from those I made as a kid.

I leaf through my journal and find an answer, sort of:

Woke at 5 a.m. today to grade my students' final research papers. Was gulping down coffee and rushing through the papers when Tessa came sleepily padding down the stairs and plopped down on the sofa next to me. She brought Snowbell, a white kitten that never stops "talking"—an unending string of mournful meows. Drives me nuts. I had 50 or so papers to finish, so I became impatient with the cat and with Tessa. Why did she wake up so early on the one day I needed to grade? She didn't pick up on my frustration however, and began to ask questions. "Whatcha doing Daddy?" "What are you writing on their papers?"

Then she came over (with the loudly meowing cat in her arms) to see for herself. She immediately focused on a grade I had just written, a C-. "Where's the other eye?" she asked. I didn't get it. "What are you talking about?" I grumped. She saw the encircled C as the smile and the minus as one eye of an incomplete "Have a Nice Day" face. Her observation startled me. I realized that I had been grading too fast, too low, and with too much attention on mechanics rather than my students' ideas. Tessa assumed that I was as affirming as her teacher, who often used stars and smiley faces.

I slowed down then—stopped tenaciously searching for run-ons and comma splices, and tried to identify the ideas or images that I thought mattered most to my students.

Tessa's comment got me thinking: Why was it so much easier for me to find the flaws than the successes in my students' papers? This made me wonder about my parenting—was I listening as poorly to my children as I was to my students?

A few weeks later I spent a day at The Cenacle, a nearby Catholic retreat center. Upon leaving, I noticed a poster in the main hallway. The poster featured a series of short sentences with dark letters overlaid against a yellow and brown watercolor wash. The stack of words is titled "Original Sin."

He is not perfect. She is not perfect. They are not perfect. I am not perfect. You are not perfect. We are not perfect. It is not perfect.

This seemed like a script from one of those *Saturday Night Live* feel-good therapy sketches. But not when I reread it a few times. The repetitive "not," the inclusion of six personal pronouns, and the enormity of the seventh—of "it"—troubled me.

The word *perfect* is often defined as flawlessness, yet a central Latin root of the word offers another less-known definition: "completeness." The perfection an artist seeks is not flawlessness, but beauty—a sense of the whole of creation captured in a tiny piece of it—in the slow curves of a melody or a sentence or in the boney "S" of the human spine.

On a radio show today I heard some TV star described as having "a perfect body." I didn't know who the host was referring to, but I knew what. Here "perfect" means thin, well-toned, clear-skinned—Barbie- or Ken-like—camera-ready for an underwear or bra commercial. Such media-driven perceptions of beauty are destructive—particularly for adolescents, whose bodies are still blooming into fullness. TV beauty is epitomized by an "extreme makeover": normal (flawed) people seeking abnormal (flawless) bodies and lives. Surgeons cut away wrinkles, suck out fat, shorten noses, inflate lips, and tuck in cheeks. Beauty is flawlessness, rather than wholeness, appearance rather than essence.

I see this everywhere. On this warm March day a man in a brown uniform is spreading fertilizer on a neighbor's lawn. Soon he will spray pesticides and herbicides from his chemical truck with his chemical hose. Then he will plant his little white flag, officially surrendering to the façade of beauty. The chemicals kill everything except the Kentucky blue grass and the Georgia rye. The "beauty" of a poison-perfect lawn is its homogeneity. It appears "healthy," but destroys plant diversity, a real sign of health. And the toxins leech into the nearby DuPage River, killing hundreds of plants and frogs and fish.

One of the menacing weeds the lawn service man kills is the dandelion. I have mindlessly dug up thousands over the years with that little tool that looks like a metal snake tongue. But I don't anymore. I just never considered that maybe the grass was getting in *their* way rather than vice versa. Why did I change my mind? Because I know when Bennett picks one and blows the seeds skyward, and watches them ride the warm currents of air through the dappled sunlight, it will fill me with awe. And then I will do it too—pluck one of the bitter milky stems with its see-through globe of seed-topped filaments and blow them back to God.

An artist seeks the beauty sleeping in everything.

I think of Rembrandt wandering the streets of Amsterdam in the sixteenth century and finding the worn, forgotten faces of old men and women, the weeds that hadn't been pulled because no one noticed them. He found and framed and painted those tired, beaten faces with such compassion that they now hang as masterpieces in museums around the world. Rembrandt, like many artists, reveals that beauty is more about difference than sameness, more about flaw than its absence.

Empty again, I return to my seeds file for inspiration and find Marvin Bell's lovely poem "To Dorothy."[14] The first two lines capture in nine words what I've been trying to say for the last few hundred:

You are not beautiful, exactly.
You are beautiful, inexactly.

Amish quilts are also inexactly beautiful. These quilts are admired for their detail and delicate craftsmanship, but a closer look shows the seamstress always intentionally sews a flaw into each one, to express the nature of humanity—flawed yet whole. And these "imperfections" add to the beauty and value of a quilt rather than detract from it.

I think this is the central idea of Lamott's books: the quilt of a human life—of a family and a faith—*requires* flaw and ambiguity and vulnerability to be complete, to be whole. The only real "advice" she ever offers for how to stitch together such a life is not new: Pay attention. "Writing can give you what having a baby can give you: it can get you to start paying attention, can help you soften, can wake you up."[15]

Art and faith are about waking up, and waking others up, again and again to the miracle of creation. The quality of my attention as a parent and writer may enable me to find God where I least expect God—in a patch of dandelions, in an old forgotten face, in a stack of my students' papers, in a child's innocent question.

SPRING

Being an artist means, not reckoning and counting, but ripening like the tree which does not force its sap and stands confident in the storms of spring, without the fear that after them may come no summer. It does come.

—Rainer Maria Rilke[1]

Lily

"And can any of you by worrying add a single hour to your span of life? If then, you are not able to do so small a thing as that, why do you worry about the rest? Consider the lilies, how they grow: they neither toil nor spin."

—Luke 12:25–27a

A half-foot of snow fell three days ago, but yesterday and today the temperature climbed into the 60s. Everything is dripping. The swampy ground nearly sucks off my tennis shoes when I walk from the farmhouse to the henhouse, where it is finally warm enough to write again. I turn on my toaster-oven space heater, sit down at my desk, pull out my seeds file, and find the obituary notice for Eleanor Busch in a recent *Maquoketa Iowa Sentinel* edition. She and her husband, Arnie, were in my dad's church and had a farm. In the fall my brother and I used to tramp through their woods. Sometimes in the winter their son, Russ, took us sledding on those long hills that sloped down to the Maquoketa River. In July or August our mom took us out to blanch, cut, and bag sweet corn for freezing. The family also had a small dairy. I loved watching Mr. Busch, a kind man who rarely spoke, hook up his cows to the milking machine, slipping their shiny udders into the plastic sheaths. For him and the cows it seemed as matter of fact as bleeding a radiator. But having milked a cow only once, and with my hands, the coupling of animal and machine enthralled me. Such were the joys of a preacher's kid in a small Iowa town.

The Busch family, like the other farmers in my dad's church, had a blood and bone connection to the land. It was a good, hard life that a father was honored to pass down to a son. But I sensed the beginning of the end of the small family farm when I entered high school. By the time I finished college, only a handful were left. Most of my friends who had planned to work their parents' farms never did. The mega farms grew and grew and finally took over. Farming became less about working with nature than *revising* it—growth hormones for livestock, genetically altered crops, computerized feeding stations, and on and on.

I confess my nostalgia, but many of the farmers I remember as a kid seemed to care as much about the land itself as how much money they could squeeze out of it. Wendell Berry aptly describes their life: "they tend to farms…small enough to know and love, using tools and methods that they know and love, in the company of neighbors that they know and love."[2] Such lives valued moderation, the idea of enough—enough land and seed, enough sun and rain. I think of Leroy and Ruth Guyer, two farmers who made a "good living" off of eighty acres of land and a couple dozen goats, though you could read a history of the weather in Leroy's face—the deep furrows winding around his eyes and running across his forehead, all plowed by a lifetime of hail and drought. Such worry among the farmers I knew was balanced by relentless backbreaking work, and a quiet, resilient faith.

Once at a potluck in the church basement Mrs. Guyer said that the first white blossoms on an apple tree each spring were the only proof she needed that there was a God. I think I would need a bit more, or maybe a little less. I don't know. I equate God less with proof than presence. Yet, I admire a farmer's faith: the certainty that the frozen tomb of winter, the plot of rock-hard soil, can be softened and nurtured again and again into a bright green sea of waving corn. The corn, like a blooming apple tree, is an ordinary miracle. But so is the whole of creation. Maybe that's the point. If we want to find the sacred, we need only look around us, at the world we are walking through.

Miracles don't contradict nature, Saint Augustine once mused, only what we *know* about nature.[3] The farmers in my dad's church knew more about nature than most people I've met since. Of course, they worried about yields and prices and set-asides; but they also had a deep understanding of creation, of how we're all connected. Calving in their barns at midnight, or slowly churning through the late spring mud on their tractors at dawn planting corn, they lived so intimately on the earth that they may have understood miracles less as aberration than as the epitome of nature.

When I see the word *miracle*, I see the first four letters—the Spanish imperative "Mira!" which I often heard while staying in Nicaragua or Guatemala (usually when someone was pointing something out to me that I had missed). It means "Look!" or "Pay attention." Miracles come to those who pay attention. We cannot consider the lilies if we cannot see them or smell them or touch them— if we don't drop to our knees.

Abby gave me a birthday present a couple of years ago that I'll never forget. She swept up a cup of dried-out geranium petals that had fallen from several plants onto the floor of our dining room. She added a couple of dried mums and some mint leaves she had picked outside, put them in a little cough drop tin, wrapped it up, and gave it to me as her homemade potpourri. I think she made it that same day, because her hands still smelled like mint and geraniums, like creation.

One root of the word *miracle* means "wonder." And as our kids teach us every day, "wonder" (them) and "worry" (Carol and I) are on opposite ends of the emotional continuum. Wonder is the sensate world of the present. Worry is the half-empty glass of the future. For me, a little faith in creation, in the apple blossom or a box of dried flowers, can help balance the two—a faith that is not blind, but that opens the eyes.

On my afternoon walk today, while the sun wheeled through the empty sky and threw its warm spokes of light through the pine trees and budding oaks, I found a patch of trout lilies blooming in the woods amid the melting snow. There was just enough light and heat to prompt the unfolding of the petals—the "grand opening" that no one else would see. From each pair of the broad mottled leaves a single green stem lifted a five-petaled flower, a curled yellow star, back to the sky.

The next day, just before I drove home to Chicago, I went to the woods to check on the lilies. The petals were dark, already folded up for the year. They only bloom for a few days. While this seems like a blink in the life of the woods, for the ants, who crawl over and around the lilies in search of a bead of dew or a shred of leaf to carry back to their queen, the blooming is a long time. It is a bit longer still for the mites and bacteria who will soon eat the flower into humus, back into the earth. To the mind of the forest and the clock of the sun, a blooming lily is one of a million silent openings each spring that says *here we are again.*

And again and again.

When I consider those Iowa farmers re-turning the soil each spring—a lifetime of planting, waiting, worrying, harvesting—I recognize what attracts me here to rural Michigan. Time is measured less by the anxiety of commerce than by the blooming of flowers and ripening of fruits and vegetables. I can better discern the rhythm of the seasons. From asparagus in May to blueberries in July to acorn squash in September, I know *what* grows *when*—what's "in season."

Modern grocery stores, however, are no longer bound by the seasons, by local climates. The miracles of global transit and hi-tech fertilization and genetic alteration mean I can buy Australian tomatoes in February or Mexican strawberries in March. These hybrids are a seductive shade of red but were picked and shipped green: durable but flavorless. The strawberries that grow here in our Michigan garden bear in June, the tomatoes in August. They are only "in season" for a few weeks; but they are ripe, deliciously sweet, worth the wait. And, as I learned from my mom and Mrs. Busch, if you want them out of season there's a solution: Mason jars. Such flavor, such a life, is worth preserving.

Though the word *season* means "time of sowing," "in season" has come to mean the time of natural fruition within a given climate. As I walk through the muddy yard to refill the bird feeders, it strikes me: To live in season means to belong to the land you're standing on, to your family and neighbors, and to find enough there. It means to consider the trout lilies, or the phlox, or the jack-in-the-pulpit, or any other wild thing that rises from the earth to bloom each spring.

Spiders

"What's miraculous about a spiders' web?" said Mrs. Arable.
"I don't see why you say a web is a miracle."
"Ever try to spin one?" asked Dr. Dorian.

—FROM *CHARLOTTE'S WEB* [4]

Four spider egg sacs cling to a wall stud near the ceiling in the henhouse. Soon the specks of spider body and teeny segmented legs will crawl out of the silken balls. I think of the famous spider story my mom read to me, and we read to our children. Near the end of the book Charlotte weaves her egg sac and then dies. Readers grow to love her, but then must watch her die alone:

> Nobody, of the hundreds of people that had visited the Fair, knew that a grey spider had played the most important part of all. No one was with her when she died. [5]

Like the mouse I once accidentally crunched in the door and the goldfinch I found in the gravel, Charlotte dies with only humans present (i.e., the readers). Yet E. B. White focuses not on her isolation, but on how a spider, an infinitesimal member of the nonhuman world of nature, plays "the most important part of all." Much of White's

73

work echoes this theme: The miracles of that world are constant, but unnoticed.

Ironically, White gave Charlotte the human capacity to reason, which somehow allowed her to understand what most humans resist believing: Death is within the cycle of life. Animals are living and dying creatures.

Throughout the book, Charlotte ingeniously prevents Wilbur, an innocent, naïve pig, from being butchered by carefully weaving words (for her human audience) into her web in the corner of the barn doorway: "SOME PIG," and, "TERRIFIC," and, "RADIANT." Hundreds of people come to see these miracles. The stunning feats convince Wilbur's owners that he is a marvel of nature, so they don't kill him. The last word Charlotte wrote in her web to impress the humans was *humble*. Templeton the rat found this word for her on a scrap of newspaper in a garbage heap. He didn't know what it meant. "Humble has two meanings," says Charlotte. "It means not proud and it means close to the ground."[6] This was the only word she wrote in her web—the only "miracle" in the story—that none of the humans ever noticed.

Nor did they notice the miracle of Charlotte's creativity. She even manufactured the raw material she wove into her lovely tapestries, in which she caught flies and grasshoppers, on which she depended to survive. Her art literally sustained her.

I look up toward the egg sacs again and notice a spider drifting in mid-air. Its abdomen is the exact size and golden color of a toasted sesame seed. Its head and thorax combined are half that size. It seems to climb down a ladder of sunlight from the ceiling, before stopping to dangle six inches from my nose. As it floats in front of me, its double-jointed needle-thin legs knit the heavy air, and I wonder: Why do these creatures inspire such fear?

At home they send my daughters running and screaming: "Spider! It's a spider, Daddy! Can you get it? But don't kill it! Please don't kill it!" The mix of terror and compassion always confuses me. Spiders kill mosquitoes, I remind them. Very few are poisonous. And what about Charlotte? Where is the threat?

The drifting spider pauses for an instant. Its legs, now completely still, look like eight little croquet wickets. Then the light changes, and I can see the line of silk streaming out of its spinneret. The glistening thread is attached to the ceiling just above my head. The spider swings on the single strand, pursuing a point of attachment.

I was surprised to read that not all spiders make webs. Only about half the 35,000 species do. I rarely notice the ones that don't, the "wandering" spiders, because the artistry of the web is what attracts me. In the woods they are often built at eye level, connecting the sassafras, redbud, dogwood, and other first-tier trees on opposite sides of the trail.

One day last fall on a trail just behind the henhouse I stumbled into a huge web. I described it in my journal:

> This morning a spider caught my entire distracted brain in its enormous web, and then abruptly crawled into my mouth (which I had opened in confusion over how to tear the sticky tangle from my face and beard). I don't think it was moving in for the kill—hoping to inject its poison in me, liquify my insides, and suck them out. Maybe, like a fisherman who has lost his bobber in the sun, the spider was lightly touching its line with a leg, "listening" for a bite, when we collided.
>
> It felt like a hairy coffee bean walking across my tongue. I scooped it out with my thumb and index finger at about the same time I figured out what it was. The spider survived what was I presume its only journey inside a human being. But it wouldn't care about that—whether I was a bumbling human, a waddling badger, or a grazing deer. And since spiders have poor eyesight (in spite of usually having eight eyes), it may have wondered where that sudden wind came from that destroyed its web and blew it into such a warm, wet cave.

My mind wanders back to Charlotte when I notice yet another cluster of egg sacs on a ceiling joist. I wonder when the sun will warm them enough for those tiny legs to start poking out, like Charlotte's offspring. I have read that book so many times that I admit I sometimes dream of being Fern, the little girl who could hear a spider talk to her. Maybe that's why I find myself listening so carefully now—to the drone of the crickets, to the slow *plip, plip, plip* of the gutter, and to the tall grass in the meadow, still dry and brittle enough to rustle in the breeze.

In the book, after Charlotte dies in late winter, her egg sacs in the barn-door frame become the promise *of spring* ("off spring") for Wilbur, the hope of life going on. Lonely, he waits and waits until Charlotte's children are finally born. And in later years, he waits each spring for her grandchildren and great grandchildren. Year after year a few of Charlotte's relatives live in the doorframe and befriend Wilbur.

The book ends with Wilbur describing this life in the barn in the years after Charlotte has died:

> It was the best place to be…this warm delicious cellar, with the garrulous geese, the changing seasons, the heat of the sun, the passage of swallows, the nearness of rats, the sameness of sheep, the love of spiders, the smell of manure, and the glory of everything.[7]

When I first read these final lines to the girls, Tessa's eyes became misty; but Abby looked disappointed: "That's the end?" she asked. "That's all!?" The book left me as it always does—lost in a moment of believing again in the glorious, ordinary cycle of things.

By mid-afternoon the temperature climbs into the 70s, warm for early May. I walk out of the henhouse into the woods and find the first orbital web I've seen this year. The sun turns it into floating concentric rings of quivering diamonds. The web's silky geometry appears more fragile than lethal. It can't, after all, catch and hold me, or a blue jay, or a flying squirrel. Yet the thick liquid that hardens into the spider's silk after leaving the spinnerets is five times stronger than steel for its weight. It is thinner than human hair yet can be stretched a quarter of an inch before breaking. *It is as strong as it needs to be.* The meticulously constructed radii and sticky spirals of the web are astoundingly effective: Freshly trapped bugs only further entwine themselves in the sticky filaments when they try to escape, ensuring their demise. It catches and holds enough flies, moths, crickets, and other bugs to provide for its maker—around thirty per day.

This is the wisdom of the spider, the quiet lesson it weaves each spring: *appropriate strength.* Enough is possible.

Enough

Be content with what you have;
Rejoice in the way things are.
When you realize there is nothing lacking,
the whole world belongs to you.

—FROM THE *TAO TE CHING*[8]

This morning the bleating of the neighbors' goats drifted in through the henhouse screens. I walked out into the meadow, and a memory I had lost decades ago returned on the wind: the smell of burning apple limbs. As a teenager I worked in a small orchard in Iowa—trimming the trees, picking up the limbs, and burning them. But the best part was the apple sorting in the old musty shed with the ancient pine floor—filling the bushel baskets with windfall johnnies and macs and paulas and winesaps. Apples and old wood smell like home to me.

My nostalgia was broken by a rusty mud-splattered tractor that came *putt-putting* down Flynn Road as if out of an old movie set. And when I looked to see who was driving, I could have sworn it was my father as a young man—the drab overalls, the straw hat, and the square shoulders thrown back—straight out of a black-and-white photo I have. We exchanged a wave, Midwestern protocol in the country.

When the tractor went over a hill and out of sight, my daydreams turned to my dad. His family raised corn and soybeans and sheep in rural Nebraska during the Depression. In those years a dust storm could block the sun and throw a summer day into darkness. Buzzing clouds of grasshoppers could destroy a section of corn in a few days. The jackrabbits were so thick that on Sunday afternoons a group of men would encircle them, herd them into a frenzied pack, and kill them with clubs.

And though it was only one generation ago, *enough* was quite a different thing in the 1930s. My parents were born into a life without electricity and indoor plumbing. Dad never had access to these amazing technologies until he went into the navy.

Enough was different in the '40s and '50s, too. My parents started a family in a place that seemed like a foreign country to them—The University of Chicago—the same campus Carol and I moved to forty years later. When my oldest brother, Robin, was born in 1949, my parents had no television or air conditioning. A "regular" drink at a soda fountain was eight ounces, and the average size of an American home was 1,000 square feet. Today the average American home is 2,200 square feet, and nearly half of those homes contain three or more color televisions. Obesity is now epidemic among America's youth, prompted in part by all those televisions, and by a "fast food" life: a super-sized, car-based, hurry-up, ultra-convenient, throw-away culture.

The small, family-owned drug and grocery stores from my childhood are as rare now as family farms. Gargantuan discount stores reveal that the world is not getting smaller, but more homogenous: a "single" theatre is now a 35–screen cineplex, a single gas station is an acre of cement with forty pumps, a single farm is not five hundred acres, but five thousand. More is always possible. Perhaps this is why numerous studies have shown that Americans, in spite of unprecedented wealth, are no more "happy" today than they were in my parents' generation.[9] We have an increasingly difficult time even imagining *mitakuye oyas'in*—that we are part of one interdependent web of life.

Today on the drive from Michigan back home to Chicago— through the sixty or seventy miles of country, small town, suburb, and city—I realized that most people will probably not take the idea of "enough" seriously until it threatens *our* survival. Only when our friends get melanoma from holes in the ozone, and our children have asthma or another air-related disease, and there is an epidemic of cholera in our town because there is no potable water will we listen to the three-legged frogs and the mercury-loaded salmon. But, then, it will probably be too late.

Here in Glen Ellyn, in the morning before I leave for work, Bennett and I often dump the coffee grounds and eggshells and orange rinds in our worm bin in the basement. Bennett likes the worms, maybe even admires them. Wriggling in dirt and slimy mashed bits of food probably seems like common sense to a two-year-old.

Maybe it is. Maybe animal instinct makes more sense than human reason. Does any creature live in a more symbiotic relationship with the earth than the red wiggler worm? These squirming nitrogen factories compensate for human excess by eating our garbage and turning it into black gold—not oil, but soil—compost. Thus, a worm bin seemed like a good way to learn something about what and how much we waste. At least that was the plan.

I initially balked at the idea of keeping our most disgusting chunks of raw garbage and great gobs of worms in a thirty-gallon plastic bin in our basement. I was shamed into it though when a "green" friend teased me about having a garbage disposal. I didn't have a good answer to his questions about waste, or about the depth of the human "footprint" on the earth. He suggested a worm bin. Carol thought it was a good idea, though she didn't seem too excited about "feeding" them.

Tessa and Abby weren't hard to convince. They had studied worms at school and shared a lot of fun facts: Just one acre of land could hold a million worms; worms have a mouth, a head and a tail, and six hearts (!), but no eyes or nose; they can sense light, and don't like it; a worm is both male and female; if their skin dries out, they'll die; the sticky slime on their bodies is full of stuff (nitrogen) that helps things grow better, as is their excrement.

Tessa and Abby did, however, take issue with my calling them "pets." A pet is warm and furry and will sleep in your bed or scurry down your shirt-sleeve. Worms are cold-blooded and slimy. I responded to their skepticism with a statistic: Worms have about 75 percent of the human genome in their makeup. We are actually pretty closely related. This didn't convince them.

When I place a worm in someone's hand, they give two responses: "yuk!" and/or "slimy!" The word's Latin root, *vermis* (i.e., vermin) suggests a noxious, quickly reproducing, disease-carrying creature. In junior high we called a kid a "worm" if he was geeky—at best quiet and insecure, at worst a social outcast. A worm is someone you can never trust—or something that could destroy a computer network. And the word is just as repugnant when used as a verb. If you "worm" your way out of a difficult situation, the implication is that you are hiding something, that you escaped by deceit.

I'm not sure why, but we decided to take the worm plunge in the dead of winter. On a bitter January afternoon, we all spent an hour outside digging through a steaming heap of rotting vegetables in a huge metal container—my college's worm bin. With the help of our biologist friends, Shamili and Glenn (long-time worm farmers) and their two children, we pulled red wiggler worms one by one from gooey chunks of broccoli and rubbery hunks of carrot. Shamili said we needed to pull at least 500 to start our plastic 30–gallon bin at home. But worms are hard to count, and after half an hour I didn't care. Did it really matter if it was 300 or 500? I was ready to leave. Yet though my hands were numb and my stomach was churning, I couldn't help but notice the worms' handiwork: The catacomb of tunnels they ate through the rotten vegetables seemed like a kind of performance art.

We took the worms home, made them a bed of damp paper fiber, fed them our waste, and they began to turn it into something good. And to reproduce! During the next week a steady stream of neighborhood kids filed into our basement to see the amazing worms. But unlike with our guinea pig and gerbil and kitten, most of the kids were satisfied with a peek and never asked to see them again. One little girl wouldn't ever go in the basement again, afraid the worms might try to "pull her into their bin."

I soon became the family worm czar, the one who fed and fretted about them. The kids learned a lesson about waste, but then they got distracted by our "real pets" and by soccer practice and homework and their friends. It is clear: I have failed in my goal of promoting worms as the perfect low-maintenance and environmentally conscious family pet. But I still love them. What other creature will eat half their weight in your trash every single day and turn it into high-grade fertilizer?

This spring, on a very warm May afternoon—73 degrees—I set the worm bin outside in the sun. It was time to harvest the compost and give the worms a fresh bed. The sun would drive the worms down deeper so I could skim off the upper layers, before removing the worms and the compost on the bottom.

The next morning I woke up shivering because our windows were still open, and I immediately knew I had forgotten. I looked at the thermometer: 40 degrees. I rushed to the patio, opened the bin and plunged my hands into the cold rotten fruit rinds and the juicy mush of a thousand dead worms.

That afternoon, still feeling sad and foolish, I dumped the bin into a flower bed and worked the worm remains in around a sickly rose bush. At first I felt the same creeping nausea in my stomach as when we had collected the worms over a year ago. But that waned when I began to consider the irony of this mass burial. How odd it was that the worms had converted me—from worm skeptic to worm advocate. Yet they could not protect themselves from my scattered mind and hurried life. And now, even in the death I had caused, they were making life, still returning more than they were given, still a part of me and everything else.

The next month, from their fertile decay, the rose bush shot skyward. The thorny branches with their crimson red blooms climbed the shutters and over the bay window in a week in their wild reach for the sun.

The Art of Faith

Religion, like poetry, is not a mere idea, it is expression.
—RABINDRANATH TAGORE[10]

In late May, while pulling the nails out of the ill-fitting storm windows inside the henhouse, I found a glass vial lying in the windowsill with a dead spider in it. It was not the spider I ate in the woods last fall, but the same species—the same size and markings. I caught it in the woods and had "filed" it for later identification. Still curious, that afternoon I took it with me to the library in Bridgman, a little town five miles north, to consult a field guide. Such guides for wildflowers or trees usually leave me baffled, providing good guesses at the species but no clear answer. This time, however, there was no question. The spider that crawled into my mouth last fall was an arrow-shaped *micrathena*—a common orb-weaver in the woods.

As I was putting the spider guide back on the shelf I was astonished to see Perry LeFevre, my first professor in seminary, slouched in one of the slick white vinyl recliners, reading the *Detroit Free Press*. I'd forgotten he and his wife had a cabin nearby. A gentle, brilliant man, nearly eighty now, he was old and bent. Yet intellectual curiosity still burned behind his eyes.

83

He remembered our class together, eighteen years earlier: "constructive theology." We read ten "seminal" books in ten weeks and then were asked to construct our own theology in thirty pages or less. I wondered why we had to take any other classes! I loved the books, the smorgasbord of theology—systematic, process, liberation, black, feminist, gay, environmental, and on and on. But I had no idea how to construct a small-town-Iowa-white-guy theology, or if I was even supposed to. The class left me reeling in theories and introduced me to the central theme of religious study: There are no good answers, but good questions are inexhaustible. You can spend a lifetime pleasantly (or horribly) tangled in a few of the best ones.

Perry had introduced me to Søren Kierkegaard's phrase "a leap of faith"—the idea that faith always involves risk—a perilous lunge from secure reason toward meaning, toward the irrational, toward God.[11] I've been thinking about that image lately, because I heard a sermon last week in which the minister seemed to view this leap as a single moment in his life—a specific day and time when he became a "believer" and was certain he had been "saved." The leap was an answer, and now he lived in a world of answers. Rather than leaping into the abyss of not knowing, his experience seemed like jumping in place.

If faith is an art, a process, the leap is not a momentary act of conversion, but a life of creativity. Art, like faith, is not about landing.

Maybe the best "answer" to the bottomless questions the artist leaps from and toward is another question. Rainer Maria Rilke, in his classic *Letters to a Young Poet*, advises an aspiring writer how to deal with this troubling uncertainty—with artistic doubt:

> be patient toward all that is unsolved in your heart and try to love the *questions themselves* like locked rooms and like books that are written in a very foreign tongue. Do not seek the answers, which cannot be given you because you would not be able to live them. And the point is, to live everything. *Live* the questions now.[12]

My dad taught me this in eighth grade. He was my confirmation teacher. Seven of us took the class—four boys and three girls. With our voices breaking up and our oily faces breaking out, my friend Craig and I tried to repress our roaring hormones for the ninety–minute Saturday morning meetings. After the eight weeks of study, we were to stand in front of the congregation on Sunday morning and answer a series of prescribed questions: Do you believe in God, Maker of heaven and earth? Do you accept Jesus Christ as your personal Savior? Do you believe Jesus is the Son of God?

I told my dad I couldn't do it, that I wasn't ready, that my gut said no. He was a bit surprised, but accepted my decision, perhaps recognizing himself in my doubts. In hindsight, I think I listened to his lessons and his life more carefully than I knew. And it boiled down to this: religious faith is not about answers. I may have taken the questions too literally, and I could have tried to answer them the way I felt. But I didn't have the confidence to try, and the expected yes or no responses just didn't seem to square with the topic at hand. I didn't want to close the questions that my dad had just opened.

They are still wide open. Though I couldn't articulate it then, the heart of my "faith" was the search for meaning in the mystery of creation. It still is. "To believe" for me is not to find the "answer," but to participate, to witness, to co-create—a family, a community, a life in art, maybe a book.

Faith is a commitment to a process of discovery.

This is the leap/life I understand. Both Tessa and Abby have already asked Carol and me the question we asked our parents: If God created us, who created God? I usually respond with both an answer ("I really don't know") and a question ("What is God?" or "Who is God?"). They think this is funny. They presume I *know*: "No, *REALLY* Dad. What's the answer?" Sometimes I say, "I wonder if those chipmunks know what or who God is?" and I'm not kidding.

While driving back to Chicago from the farm, I saw a bumper sticker on the interstate that I have seen before: "Jesus is the answer." I always wonder what the question is. Such faith, a faith of answers, bothers me not only because it excludes other religions and interfaith dialogue, but because it shuts down the inherent creativity of Christianity, the art of faith, and thus gives it a bad name.

That night my writing group met and critiqued one of my essays, which dealt in part with the problem of defining God. Toward the end of our discussion, Roberta, a writing teacher, thought I was a bit evasive, so she asked an honest question. "What *do* you think about God and faith?"

The next week at the farm I take a crack at Roberta's question. I start by digging in my seeds file and find this from Wendell Berry:

> Creation is not in any sense independent of the Creator, the result of a primal creative act long over and done with, but is the continuous constant participation of all creatures in the being of God.[13]

I like his idea of "constant participation," but how do I capture it with ink and paper? If I had a "present tense/sense" hyperlink on the top of this page to transport readers here, now, to the henhouse, maybe I could get it right.

A storm is blowing in from Lake Michigan: first the hushing whisper of the white pine, and then the wild to-and-froing of the cottonwood leaves. Finally a blue-gray tidal wave of cloud buries the sun and rolls the woods into deep, cool shadow.

God is the heavy sweetness I taste blowing through the screens, the low rumble behind the trees, the cracking zigzags of light that slash at the earth.

A few soft arrows of rain shoot here and there, before growing into the barrage I love. It pelts down like the fistfuls of gravel we used to heave at the black-tarred roof of our old elementary school at recess, back when we were still curious about the sound of gravity.

The brown grass blows and tosses in the rain and drinks and drinks and dreams and dreams of God, and is God.

Then I hear Roberta's question. How can I make such a claim with certainty?

I can't. I look out the window. A robin is bathing under the eave, primping in the rusty spillover of a leaf-jammed gutter. As soon as he finishes aligning his feathers and pulling that worm from the ground, I decide I'm going to ask *him*. Maybe he knows what God is, what it is these words will never touch.

I teach a weekly English as a second language course at a local church in Glen Ellyn—an informal class of nine Mexican immigrants: seven women and two men. They walk from a nearby apartment building. The church furnishes childcare. We do not give grades. We work hard and have fun. Today, I bring in pots and pans and food to teach cooking vocabulary.

Lupe grabs the spoon and says, "This is *cuchillo*."

"What is it in English?" I ask. She is uncertain, but thinks hard. When I start to talk, she smiles, holds up her open hand, and lightly says, "*Esperate. Esperate.*" I wait.

"Spuhnnn. Spuhn," Lupe says. "Spoon," Alberto corrects.

I smile and nod, but I'm confused. I know *esperate* as the imperative form of *esperar*, but from her tone she seemed to mean "Wait," and I remember *esperar* as meaning "to hope." Yet I can't imagine her commanding me to "Hope!"

I later check my Spanish-English dictionary. *Esperar* does have two meanings—"to wait" and "to hope."

When I think of waiting and hoping, now I think of faith. And it strikes me as odd that, unlike *hope* and *wait,* the word *faith* doesn't have a verb form. If I had to choose a verb, I think I would pick "to believe."

Curious, I pull out my *Oxford English Dictionary* and look all three verbs up:

To hope: "the expectation of a desire"; to wait: "to remain"; to believe: "to hold dear."

The overlay of these three definitions helps me understand how faith and art might intersect—why artists wait and hope hour after hour and year after year poised in front of a canvas or a piano or a computer screen in patient expectation of beauty, of the holy.

Artists wait because they hope to create what they believe. And they may discover what they believe in the process of creation. For me, waiting and hoping and believing are not preliminary steps to making art, but are the heart of art, and of faith—essential and constant. Most artists I know struggle to keep going, to believe in their work, or even to believe that they are artists. I do. Hope enables me to choose art, to live a life of patient expectation.

I see the process of art as "religious" then, because I see this creative hope and work as an attempt to belong to the Whole, to what I call God. Believing enables belonging. To "hold dear" the Creator is to "hold dear" the creation.

I go up and sit in the dining room near an open window. The crickets are singing. A raccoon (or is it a possum?) tries to work the lid off our trash can. A car full of screaming high school kids roars by. The Siberian husky across the street starts to howl. At what, I don't know. Now he's pulling and jangling his metal chain. Perhaps he is hungry, or saw the raccoon, or wants to come inside. A few minutes later he stops. I wonder if they let him in, of if he is simply tired and has laid down in the grass to sleep.

I go up to bed and lie down next to Carol, who is reading a novel. She looks over her glasses with a smile that means, "Hi, isn't it great to have a few quiet minutes to read?" I flick on my light and pick up an essay from my nightstand that I've been wanting to reread. Chris, a student in an English composition class, wrote it last year. I called him this week because I remembered his paper included an artful analogy related to faith, and I wanted to read it again. Here is the introduction:

> Grasping hold of a cottonwood seed is not easy. The white fiber antennae of the seed hover and float through the soft, unseen currents of air. A drop in altitude is countered by an upward thrust, paradoxically keeping the seed both in constant turmoil and continual stability. Attempting to catch a falling cottonwood seed can seem futile. The seed is so delicate that the slightest motion toward it disrupts its path, sending it scurrying away. It is not until one stops pursuing the seed and simply opens his hand to the sky, like a child receiving a gift, that the falling cottonwood seed will come to rest on his palm.

Chris's image helps me understand the art of faith, or reminds me that I can't. I lie there imagining an empty, open hand, patiently waiting in the sunlight. Then I dream of the thousands of seeds, those quiet prayers, that are riding the wind through the darkness right now. Soon they will come to rest somewhere. And they, too, will wait—for a soft blanket of dust, and a shiny coat of rain. When their world softens, they will sink into the soil and try to grow, to push their way through the rocky earth.

SUMMER

Homing

The henhouse is hot and muggy this afternoon. I sip on a tinkling glass of ice water and try to regain my focus. I can hear the distant whine of semi trucks on Interstate 94, the pipeline back to Chicago, and an owl hooting off in the woods. Each sound points to its own wilderness, and the paradox of progress. After my short stays here, I always long to return to Carol and the kids, but not to metro Chicago.

We have lived in or near Chicago for seventeen years, though I have never felt at home there. Not in the city, nor the inner ring of suburbs, nor the far western suburb where we now live. Some restless pull won't let go of me. It's not the "grass is always greener" mind-set. And I'm not another white goose in that great gaggle of "traitors" who flew west to evade urban struggles. It's more basic than that. I'm not *from* there.

Even during the years we lived in a rice farming community in the Philippines—without a car or phone, or reliable electricity—a part of me felt more at home there than in Chicago.

I know the reason: I grew up in Iowa. Somehow, I never accepted the concrete gridlock and human density of the city. The myriad of choices and frenetic energy tire rather than inspire me. While Glen Ellyn is actually a small town that sprang up just after the Civil War, it is now part of an immense network of older communities and new "developments" that are gobbling up meadow, forest, and farmland at a disturbing rate. Everything is connected by a tangle of eight-lane arteries clogged 24/7 with millions of cars on their way to 50–acre malls and 100–acre parking lots, or to cookie-cutter split-level ranch subdivisions, or to gated enclaves of five-bedroom brick mansions, or, most likely, to a fast-food establishment.

"Go west, young man." Carol and I keep moving—every five or six years we drift another ten or twenty miles west. First it was Hyde Park on the city's south side, then Oak Park on the city's western boundary, now a western suburb. Perhaps the next stop is Sycamore, a little town still floating in the cornfields. After Sycamore, if we can accelerate our migration to fifty miles every five years, we should make the Rochelle area about the time we turn fifty, Dixon around sixty, and dip our hands in that great blue boundary, the Mississippi River, around our seventieth birthdays. I'm on a slow, sedulous journey back to Iowa.

I'm not sure why I'm so restless. In spite of how much I love the henhouse and the woods behind it, the quiet grasp of memory won't let me go: the lingering desire to bale hay, walk beans, or set a trot line for bullhead in some muddy pond. And I'd still trade a foamy latte at the megamall for a chipped cup of joe in some little Iowa town. The Iowans I knew were pragmatic and frugal. They tried to fix things before they threw them away. They cared about their tools and knew how to use them. They bought trucks with four-wheel drive not to take their kids to soccer practice, but to get though the mud. I think I long for Iowa because I long for less, for a less "developed" world. I find some of this in Bridgman and Sawyer and the little towns near the farm, but the pull of childhood is not rational. It pulls on the heart.

By late afternoon it cools off, but I have run out of words. The rush of ideas that I woke with has diminished to a trickle. A ruby-throated hummingbird stops by at dusk, beating the soft light into a familiar hum. He is trying to find nectar somewhere in the screen-door frame—probably smells my ripe cantaloupe rind. He hovers near a stud, pauses at the shiny handle, and then darts away. Night arrives soon after he leaves. I gather my books and clothes, pack the car, and head down the long dark highway back to Chicago.

Two weeks later, rather than driving east to Michigan, to the farm, I drive west to Iowa, to help my parents with a painting project in their home. But first I'll stop in Maquoketa, my hometown, the place I come from. I want to test my nostalgia, to see if that little town is really the utopia I imagine.

I rocket out of Chicago on Interstate 88 past dozens of sparkling corporate headquarters and megastores, through fifteen miles of sprawling new housing developments. These subdivisions are called Blackberry Crossing, Silver Leaf Glen, Amber Fields, and Willow Walk Homes—suggesting a slow, simple, pastoral life. The key considerations, however, seem to be ready access to a golf course, a shopping mall, and an interstate entrance ramp. People don't walk through the neighborhood here.

In a half hour, hayfields divided by winding creeks and small stands of trees appear—the wilds of the Midwest. I begin to wonder if a suburb or city is any less "natural" than the pesticide-drenched farms I worked on as a kid, and now romanticize. Oddly, I see as much wildlife in "Chicagoland" as in the Iowa wood lots I once roamed. A week ago we discovered a red fox sunning himself in our backyard and sniffing out the bird feeder.

Raccoons waddle through our forsythia like furry tanks. Possums dangle from our elm trees at night. The skunks have figured out how to work the bungee cord off our plastic trash can. A family of coyotes lives in a patch of woods near the new strip mall. All these creatures seem as certain they belong in the 'burbs as we do. Their one-time wooded homes farther west—the land I'm buzzing through—are now muddy, new subdivisions. Their displacement, their search for home, is real, about survival. Mine isn't.

Soon I am cruising through central Illinois—past thousands of acres of corn stubble and slow strings of cows plodding back to their barns. It looks a lot like Iowa, and parts of Michigan. A friend who is always rushing through these plains on his way to somewhere beautiful asks me why I like it so much here. Is it, he asks, because I've never been to the mountains or the ocean or the north woods? I usually get a little embarrassed and a little defensive. He's teasing. But I don't have a good answer.

Twice, somewhere in the middle of the state, near the turn off for Dixon, I see red-tailed hawks stoically perched on fence posts. Unlike humans, these stern, tufted sentinels don't rely on reason. A red-tail doesn't wonder where it belongs. It kites on a thermal. It dives at the earth like a stunt plane to snatch a vole resting in a meadow. The vole, five ounces of fur and blood, is not a moral dilemma.

Perhaps my homing in on Iowa, on "the country," is not simply nostalgia, but an odd remnant of human instinct—a vestige from the days when our ancestors belonged to the earth rather than possessed it, when we read the world as creation rather than commodity.

This morning in Glen Ellyn I watched a flock of warblers flying south and felt envious. A third of them were flying to a "home"—a feeding and mating ground—they *know* without having ever seen it before. The human sensory system cannot use the sun or stars or the earth's magnetic pulls as a precise internal map. Yet, maybe our homing is also a kind of coping strategy. The goal is not food, nor physical, but spiritual. We are searching for where we belong. My problem is that it rarely seems to be where I am.

Now, in the distance, a cloud of synchronized black flecks, sparrows, drop out of nowhere and then abruptly and beautifully change direction, like a fistful of pepper caught in a swirl of wind. The uniform airborne shifts, the instinctive choreography, is a work of art. In the rearview mirror the moon brightens into a faint orange globe, seeming to absorb the light that bleeds from the cool air. The western sky ahead is a pink and maroon river of cloud that swirls toward its mouth, the red lake of the sun, which soon seeps beneath the horizon, the only hard line left in the world.

As I hum through the membrane of light that separates night and day, I think of Thoreau's journal, *Walden*, which I just taught. I'm always amazed how a book written in the middle of the nineteenth century, before electricity and cars and indoor plumbing, can be so current, so predictive of the risks of unbridled technology and affluence. When my freshman composition class discussed "Economy," the long first chapter of *Walden*, we considered the infamous "desperation" sentence, as my classes always do. But this time around, I was struck by the less-known lines that follow it:

> The mass of men lead quiet lives of desperation. What is called resignation is confirmed desperation. From the desperate city you go to the desperate country, and have to console yourself with the bravery of minks and muskrats.[1]

I think of my own desperate migrations between city and country and the "courage" of the animals who are desperately trying to survive alongside the most destructive species in their habitat—human beings. The Latin root of *desperate* means "without hope." Yet the word has also come to mean "frantic" and "dangerous." Perhaps in today's culture of accumulation, *desperate* also means "the inability to be satisfied." I often wonder if Thoreau's contentment had more do with belonging, with his ability to be satisfied, than with a particular location. His personal economy of shovels and nails and seeds stemmed from his love for the natural economy in the woods and water surrounding him. He saw the connections. He knew that home is where *enough* is.

I cross another hill. A tree by the road blows and shakes in the new moonlight. I imagine the enormous network of roots below ground, probing the soil for water. Wendell Berry once wrote that trees are "immobile yet flexible." They grow and adapt even though fixed in the dirt. They bloom where they are planted.

People seldom do. Few are planted at all. We increasingly associate "success" with mobility and accessibility, with more. We can work and live anywhere with a laptop and a cell phone. Starbucks™ has become the corporate office for an army of entrepreneurs. Last week I tried to drink my cup of Sumatra and read *The New York Times* in one of those big cushy chairs, while the guy next to me chattered with a client about his stock portfolio. Soon he was glaring at me as if I should find something more important to do.

Roots have become a liability. Having long admired the Amish community in Iowa, I once visited an even more traditional one, in Lancaster County, Pennsylvania. During an afternoon drive through the countryside I noticed two boys pushing themselves down a long dirt road on kick scooters. "They can't have bikes," my friend, who grew up in Lancaster County, explained. "An Amish council determined that the chain and sprocket was too high-tech." It could break down community, too easily draw people away from their families and homes, from their roots. While this admittedly seems a bit dictatorial, I admire the central ethic: community over convenience, sustenance over satiation.

My wheels roll into the darkening night. The stars brighten in the distance, conjure a universe. As I crane my neck to find the moon through the windshield, I wonder if it is my desire for something else, something more, that gilds the memory of "home," of Iowa, as paradise.

In my desk I have a small black shard of a fossilized turtle shell someone once gave me. Every time I look at it I remember I could decide to belong, to be at home, *anywhere*. And yet I often long to be somewhere else—somewhere slower, smaller, more wild, somewhere where a moment can slowly open in the sunlight and last all day. I long to be where I'm not. I long to be. I long.

The drone of my engine puts me in a trance: longing… being…longing…being…belonging… I crank the window down. The cool must of wet hay from someone's barn awakens childhood. Two farmhouses lit up in the distance reveal the bluffs that line the Mississippi. It has taken two hours to cross Illinois. In the darkness, on the bridge over the river, I remember what Mr. Streets, my high school math teacher, told me as I left for college: "Some day you'll miss this little town you now want to escape." He was right. Our home does not belong to us; we belong to our home. Things change. Memory misleads.

Now in Iowa, I continue over the river bluff toward Davenport. I see a smattering of lights nearby. A yellow Caterpillar™ slowly crawls through the mud. As it digs out a basement its headlights illuminate the wooden skeleton of a new home. Even from the highway I can make out the warm breath of steam rising from the fresh gash in the earth. A new subdivision. Suburban Iowa.

A few miles later a detour leads me to a two-lane black top that winds through the low hills. I've never gone this way before. I honor the 25 m.p.h. speed limit in a one-gas-station, one-bank, three-bar town. In five minutes I'm in the country again and lost. I decide to follow a direction, west, rather than the map, and see what happens.

I turn onto a gravel lane and drive until I don't see any cars. I slow, pull onto the dirt shoulder, climb out, and stand next to my door—a bewildered pilgrim. Why does this feel like sacred ground?

I stare into the night expecting to recognize something, but don't. It is quiet. A light in someone's barnyard, a sparkling sea of stars, and a full moon are bright enough that a cottonwood along the road casts a slight shadow. A stiff wind blows through the grass, bends the sumac, jostles the goldenrod. I pull back onto the gravel road and head toward where I think the highway should be. And then, after a few miles, I miraculously hit it—Highway 61—the road home. It is four lanes now, rather than two.

Maquoketa, where I grew up, is the Jackson County seat—around 6,000 people. The first thing I notice upon arriving is that the little red light on the top of the water tower no longer marks the town at night. Rather, a startling eighty-foot-high sign topped by red-and-yellow arches burns in the night sky. The family-run Flapjack Restaurant across the street is dark and empty. The bank sign next to it says "God less America": the capital "B" has fallen from its plastic rails.

I soon discover that the old bowling alley and the cornfield behind it are now a Wal-Mart™ and a five-acre parking lot. Clearly the liveliest spot in town on Saturday night, it is still crowded at 9 p.m. Curious, I park and head into the store. I spy a metal *Des Moines Register* paper rack in front. A front page story, "Bush Combats Terror at Home," claims the most patriotic thing Americans can do to help fight the war on terror is to go shopping. I whoosh inside.

A bent gray-haired man in a blue vest, an "associate," welcomes me and gives me a cart. Most of the little family-run stores I loved on Main Street have gone out of business. They are here now, all displaced into one convenient megastore: pets, hardware, groceries, appliances, sporting goods, clothing, shoes, plants and trees, auto supplies, and a pharmacy.

The lines in the fifteen checkout lanes are long, but no one is using the self-scan lane. The "guests" prefer people to machines. I wander deeper into the linoleum maze—past the precariously stacked display towers of lemon-scented kitty litter and portable grills, then along a wall of ten thousand shoes and tissue boxes and laundry baskets. The Lionel Ritchie song on Muzak™ is interrupted for the announcement of a "price rollback" on hazelnut decaf 32 ounce cans: $2.99.

I don't know what to buy or why I've come here. I should head over to Iowa City to my parents' place, but I find it difficult to leave. The store is familiar; and as I stumble along, I feel both a bit sad and oddly at home. When I sit down in a wooden pine rocker in the home furnishing section, another price rollback blares through the store in a digitized voice: twelve four-ounce packs of corn chips for $3.99. I rock back and forth in the fluorescent light and dream of my family back in Chicago, where I belong. Here, in the place I come from, I watch my fellow Iowans, as they quietly thread themselves through the shiny grid of aisles and the cardboard display bins, through a world of choices.

Something Enormous

This is the day they said would never come
and now it seems will never end.
This is the day the heart cannot believe,
that eyes cannot take in. This is the day we must begin.
This is the day when no one knows what to say,
when prayers and cries become one and the same,
when silence begins where language ends.
This is the day we will never forget, this the day we
*   must begin.*

—Jim Moore[2]

Today is Bennett's third birthday. We had a little party in the backyard this afternoon—cake and ice cream with some of the neighborhood kids. They were all older, Tessa and Abby's friends, but they were kind, and seemed as excited by the event as Bennett was.

They played "Duck, Duck, Goose." When Abby tapped Bennett's head, his little determined body sprang up and sprinted off in a different direction, not around the circle. Abby chased him around the yard, caught him, and they both fell down laughing. Later he blew out his three candles, ate his chocolate ice cream in the sun, and let it drip down his face onto his shirt. I watched him run out into the yard after a rubber ball, indifferent to the brown sticky mess, to everything but the red ball on the green grass in the summer sun.

His innocence pushes me to tears and fills me with hope. Three years. Some days it feels like a blink, and others like a lifetime. We have been parents for ten years. I can barely remember our life without children, a life where I wasn't so lifted up and so weighted down, so blessed and so utterly confused, so stunned by wonder and stung by worry. Somehow the first few months of Bennett's life epitomized this paradox, the art of a family. The birth itself was a moment that never really ended, that we still carry.

He was born on a hot July day around 6:30 p.m., just twenty-five minutes after we arrived at the hospital. I had barely helped Carol roll out of her wheelchair and onto the bed before he was crowning. Our midwife, Therese, then gently placed my hands on the almond-shaped crest of his head. "You can catch him," she told me. I hadn't yet adjusted to the shock of her words when my hands felt the small wet patch of hair and scalp grow into a purple-blue orb, with a face, that soon began to grimace. Still malleable, slightly flattened by the exit muscles, our son's head was in my hands.

Then, from that deep coupling of pain and joy, Carol gave one last amazing push; and like billions of mammals before him, Bennett glided out of the dark, warm cocoon of muscle in a bloody gush of water. In that moment of both separation and union he both left and arrived home. As he slipped into my amazed hands and into the dry, air-conditioned world of fluorescent light, his arms, which were plastered to his torso like little wings, quickly unfolded and began to flap. Then Therese laid him on Carol's stomach, where the lost, waving arms magically found intention, beginning their lifelong reaching— for love, and other things.

That night the three of us lay together on a fold-out bed in the hospital room. Bennett nursed and slept while Carol and I, in a sleep-defiant euphoria, marveled over the birth and reminisced about the births of our other children. After falling in and out of sleep for several hours, I woke at dawn to Bennett's cry. A nurse came in to check Carol's pulse and temperature. While they talked, I scooped up our son, opened the curtains, and watched the sun rise over an unmowed field.

As the lights began to wink on in the rows and rows of ranch-style houses below us, I rocked Bennett in the flooding sunlight and wondered about all those families starting their day: the beeping alarm clocks, the steaming showers, the dripping coffeemakers, the rustling newspapers, the children padding down the hallway to the bathroom. I imagined all those parents—the singles, the happily partnered, the soon-to-be separated—all struggling to make a family work. I imagined folding diapers, wiping off counters, moving stacks of letters and bills and art projects off the kitchen table for breakfast before pulling out boxes of cold cereal and a loaf of bread. Then, while the kids ate, perhaps they would lay out a row of bread slices, swipe on peanut butter and jam, shuffle them into sandwiches, plastic wrap them, and drop them in little brown bags with an apple and a juice box.

Some parents move through the daily routines of a family in joy and gratitude, others in the autopilot of exhaustion, and still others, in quiet desperation. But most, I assume, like me, have cycled in and out of all these feelings at one time or another.

The next few weeks were predictably hard—little sleep, short tempers—more exhaustion than euphoria. As parents, we never quite figured out how to keep track of a third kid, how to switch from a man-to-man to a zone. We still haven't.

Two months later, on a crystal blue September morning, Bennett was in the kitchen with me, cooing and rocking in his bouncy chair. I was doing what I usually do—wiping down the counters, emptying the dishwasher, and drinking strong coffee. Carol and Tessa and Abby were at the front door, sorting the backpacks for school. Through the open kitchen window our maple tree was already burning red and pink on the edges. The mums were blooming: small bursts of yellow and purple against the black dirt and dried grass along the back fence line. A sparrow and a cardinal chirped their complaints from the plastic lip of our empty birdfeeder. *Where's that sack of birdseed?* I thought to myself. *Did I leave it in the shed again?* Then I turned on the radio. The hour that followed has never really ended.

First, I picked up Bennett and pulled him close. Unsure whether to tell Carol and the girls, I quietly slipped upstairs with Ben to watch the TV coverage. It was on every station. The first jet plowed into the north tower in a slow motion replay. Then the second jet ripped into the south tower. Then they replayed both. I had to sit down. I imagined all those people inside, starting their day, sipping their fresh cups of coffee, and reviewing their list of tasks to complete. Perhaps one or two had looked up to watch the lazy drift of a cloud against the clear sky in that precious moment just before the plane penetrated the water-smooth panels of window.

Carol called up from downstairs that she was leaving to walk the girls to school. It didn't register. "O.K.," I yelled, after the door had already slammed. On the TV they cut to live footage—back to life as a cruel sci-fi film—and the south tower fell. A few minutes after the north tower toppled, a reporter in Washington was already feeling reflective: "This morning we learned that Americans are human," he said. "And that humans are vulnerable."

As I watched, the soft rhythm of Ben's breath warmed my neck. He wasn't sad or angry or confused. What did he fear? The loud, abrupt churning of the coffee grinder, or waking up in his crib after a nap with no face there to meet his. What could he know? Some colors, darkness and light, warmth and coldness, the emptiness of hunger, and the sheltered sweetness of his mother's breast. He didn't know hate.

When he started to coo again, the slow, unnamed wave of fear I was riding started to subside. At that moment, in a world as innocent as a little baby and as merciless as the sudden massacre of thousands, human vulnerability seemed less like flaw or weakness to me than a difficult gift, evidence of a fragile, essential connection.

But in the months after the planes hit, when the predictable and ordinary were supposed to be cause for celebration, I struggled to find solace in such routines. Perhaps because I always had before, or wanted to—wanted to believe that a parent's litany of tasks to complete could lend order and purpose to the blur of hours, to the swell of duty, to a life. But now I wasn't sure. I had lost the present tense. Thus, I questioned the gurus of mindfulness who claimed that the ordinary was sacred, that washing dishes is a form of prayer. I still admired their focus on awareness, but I had lost their faith.

I had just turned forty, and suddenly, in the emotional grip of 9/11, in that hour that felt like the brutal end of something I couldn't quite define, I was groping. So was Carol, although she was more balanced, better able to live in the present, to hold Bennett as a balm of hope. I could sometimes, but other times I was so overwhelmed by the responsibility of a new baby on top of what used to be our "normal" life that I began to lament the future—tomorrow—both in the chaotic world of our home and in the wider war-torn world Bennett would inherit.

We countered fear and frustration by going to peace demonstrations and solidarity meetings at the local mosque, by writing letters to local papers. But eventually our anger at the war and growing militarism gave way to a deep sadness. We returned to our routines. We raked the leaves and mowed the lawn and dragged out the garbage, scooped the cat's litter box, and vacuumed. We read the newspaper and paid bills and went to meetings and tried to keep up with our jobs. We took the kids to piano lessons and gymnastics and birthday parties. We dreamt and worried and argued and laughed. We went to church and poetry readings in search of something to believe in. We didn't always find it. Or happiness.

At the time I didn't recognize the impact of Bennett's birth and 9/11 on my psyche. But somehow the old self-absorbed drivenness I had in college took hold again—the always wanting something else, something more—the certainty I was not doing enough, or at least not what I was supposed to be doing. As I became more depressed, I grew impatient. And that year our marriage, like everything else, grew more fragile, more uncertain than it had in a long time. Like the half circle of elm trees that tightly framed our backyard, Carol and I stood too close together, entangled, unable to find our own way to the light we needed.

But while things fell apart, thankfully, we kept talking—staying up late, telling stories, laughing, crying, and drinking red wine. "Do you remember the rally in Chinandega?" Carol asked on one of these nights. We both laughed and then simultaneously started "the chant": "*Aquí, allá, un yanqui morirá.*" We had barely arrived in Nicaragua that summer when we attended a Sandinista rally in a small town— the only non-Nicaraguans there. Most were in green fatigues and toting AK-47s, including women and teenagers. They all started marching and chanting, and we eagerly joined in. But neither of us knew what we were saying until we had repeated it a few times. And then we got it: "Here, there, a Yankee will die." Startled, I looked around me at the sea of green soldiers, and then at Carol, with one of those "What in the hell are we doing here?" looks. It was funny even then. A woman marching next to us sensed our confusion at the irony of the chant, smiled at us, and gave Carol a pat on the shoulder. She knew why we were there, and so did we—to support their revolution and resist the U.S. attempt to bring it down.

Two weeks later we were married by Uriel Molina, a Sandinista priest, in his church in Barrio Riguero. I still remember how the cool shadows of the empty chapel that day quenched the dusty heat of the Managua street. Padre Uriel read the traditional passage from Corinthians and then one from Paul's letter to the Romans: "Do not be conformed by this world but be transformed by the renewal of your mind." After the vows he grabbed both of our hands: "The gift of your love offers you both solace and courage," he said.

That night, as we retold the stories of that summer—the quiet wedding, the Christian base communities in the banana field, the iguana we ate out of courtesy, the parasites, and the week-long downpours—we re-membered ourselves and our passions. And I began to wonder what it all meant now, eighteen years later. What claim did such stories, those people and experiences, still have on us in a suburban life of mini-vans and megamalls? I was wondering something we've often wondered—the same thing we did in that Sandinista rally that day: "What are we doing here?" It's another way of asking, "What really matters?"

This was the unspoken question at the heart of those meandering late-night talks, the question that broke us apart, and open. At times I was unsure if we were on the verge of catastrophe or enlightenment. Yet, it was only in this state of vulnerability that we recovered enough of the creative power of our love to heal.

Love heals. This is what I most remember about that time now, as I pick up the crumpled wrapping paper left from Bennett's birthday party and make my way through the familiar darkness of our home. Everyone is asleep. It's hot and still. I climb the creaky, oak stairs to our bedroom, turn on the overhead fan, and sit down lightly next to Carol. The ebb and flow of her breathing is a comfort. I watch the rhythm of her body at rest and think of her giving birth to Bennett—of his vulnerability, and ours. I replay that moment in my mind's eye as I have so many times: that first reaching out, that primal act of love between newborn and mother. It is the one moment that reminds me we are still someone's children, still naked and squirming, still a tiny, beautiful part of something enormous, still trying to find our way home.

On Saving the World

Judge them, if you must, by what they settled for. But do not mistake it for what they imagined.

—JAMES RICHARDSON[3]

Friday night. I arrive home from a meeting just before "lights out" but in time to read a chapter of Tessa and Abby's newest book: *Small Steps.*[4] It's the true story of twelve–year-old Peg Kehret's recovery from polio in a small Minnesota town just after World War II. At the end of tonight's chapter, Peg's fever has broken, and her mom and dad bring her a large brown packet of letters from her classmates at school. The letters make her reflective: "I had a strange feeling that I was reading about a different lifetime…none of this mattered. I had faced death. I had lived with excruciating pain and with loneliness and uncertainty about the future. Bad haircuts and lost ball games would never bother me again."[5]

The insight of the last line surprises me. The books I've read to the girls lately have been heavy on plot and short on theme. I read the last sentence again and ask them what they think she means. "Different things matter now," Abby says. Tessa agrees: "Yeah, and *she's* different too."

They beg for another chapter, but not tonight. I remind them that tomorrow is the last Saturday of the month, the day we collect water for a Sierra Club study of the DuPage River. They don't want to go. Way too early. Way too much car time. I promise donuts and chocolate milk on the way to the first site, and they are persuaded.

So, at 7 a.m. the next day we gather the metal pail, 25 feet of light rope, a thermometer, a roll of masking tape, a black marker, and three glass quart bottles. We stop for our high-sugar breakfast and then head out to the three assigned sites on the west branch of the river. The DuPage is slow and shallow, rarely more than twenty feet across. Each of our collection sites is five miles further west from our home. One is in a town, one in a subdivision, and one on the edge of the country.

When we arrive at the first bridge, the girls forget everything and run down the grassy incline to the dirt bank. I follow. They throw in sticks and handfuls of oak leaves to see what the moving water will do with them. Soon, we retrieve our bucket, climb up on the bridge, walk out to the middle, tie the rope to the heavy wire handle of the steel bucket and drop it down for a "clean" sample. They love the wild unraveling of the rope as the bucket drops and the tinny, hollow *kerplunk* it makes when it hits the water, fifteen feet below. The distant pull of the current on their hands shocks and delights them. How can a gallon or two of water dangling on the end of a rope be so heavy? We pull the bucket up. Abby pours a sample in the jar, measures the temperature, and considers the clarity. Tessa records the time and date. After repeating the procedure at the next two sites, we deliver all three samples to the tester, who will do the chemistry work-up.

Sometimes, after we collect a sample, the girls want to stay longer—to wander, to look for frogs, or poke a stick in a school of minnows to make them shift directions. I feel the pull of these rituals from my own childhood and am disappointed that my motivation to collect the samples has become so narrow, so pragmatic. I want to make a difference, and I want our kids to want to make a difference. The Sierra Club's ongoing study shows that the DuPage River is poisoned with phosphorous from fertilizer and treatment-plant run-off. Thus, it is choked with algae, the oxygen levels have dropped, and aquatic life is threatened.

Last week, when I gave the girls a newspaper article explaining all of this, they weren't interested. I began to summarize the article for them, and they rolled their eyes and laughed. I finally got it: They would rather read the river itself. They learn by exploring. This is a lesson they have taught me over and over: the best way to "save the world" is to belong to it, heart and soul. Political activism of any sort can feel pretty empty if all that matters is "results," if the means isn't as important as the ends.

I think I first learned this lesson as a sophomore at the University of Iowa. Obsessed with the anti-nuclear arms movement, I called Congresspeople, canvassed door-to-door for money and signatures, organized conferences, and attended endless meetings. I thought of little else and soon got involved at the national level. Once, after a demonstration in Washington, D.C., a group of us from eastern Iowa walked over to the Soviet Embassy to try and meet directly with their ambassador. We wanted to present the Nuclear Weapons Freeze Proposal and a few thousand signatures from Iowa. To our shock four of us were soon buzzed in through all the iron gates and found ourselves sitting in an office with Surgei Divilkov, the Soviet ambassador. He offered us coffee and proceeded to read the proposal. Fifteen minutes later he said he admired it and thought his government agreed with it. He thanked us for coming and encouraged us to work for an end to the arms race.

At the time I thought we had made a difference, that we had helped save the world from imminent destruction. But other than a short story in *The Washington Post*, I don't really know what it accomplished. The arms race kept escalating, and a friend later told me that the ambassador wasn't sincere, that he was using us as pawns. "Activists are often victims of their own idealism," my friend claimed. Though I sometimes wondered about my motivations and drivenness, I couldn't accept such cynicism, nor condemn idealism as a character flaw.

One winter night that same year, while editing "Peace by Peace," (a Freeze newsletter) in my apartment, I folded my arms and lay down my head to rest on a warm, humming typewriter. An hour or two later I opened my blurry eyes to a quote from Thomas Merton I had typed just before falling asleep: "Do not depend on the hope of results…face the fact that your work will apparently be worthless and even achieve no result at all…As you get used to this idea, you start to concentrate not on the results but on the value, the rightness, the truth of the work itself."[6]

The quote comes from Merton's letter to Jim Forest, a young peace activist in the 1960s. I had typed it but not understood it. Now I did. It was a wake-up call. Not only couldn't I save the world, I couldn't even *see* it. This is what I'm now trying to relearn from my kids—how to see the world.

"If I were alone in the desert and feeling afraid," writes Meister Eckhart, "I would want a child to be with me. For then my fear would disappear, and I would be made strong."[7]

Children often quell our fears with their raw honesty and constant attentiveness. They heal and inspire us not by distracting us from our loneliness, from our "lives of quiet desperation," but by attracting us back to who we were meant to be. They renew our capacity to listen to the world and to each other. They give us courage.

Lying on my desk at home is a black-and-white war photo from Sarajevo titled "Child with Gun." A wide-eyed, half-smiling little boy stands innocently next to a soldier, who is cropped out above the waist. We see only the soldier's camouflage pants tucked into his black leather boots. His large hand balances an AK-47 on end between them. The boy is exactly as tall as the rifle. Not able to reach the soldier's hand, he lightly grasps the stock of the gun as a way to "touch" the adult next to him. Unaware what impact he may have, his tiny hand on the weapon, at least for the moment, prevents it from being used. In his naiveté, it seems he doesn't recognize the danger of the gun, the violence it symbolizes, nor that he is making peace. The gunstock is all there is to hold onto, and the child's smile suggests he trusts that the soldier will somehow hold onto him, take care of him. But who is the faceless soldier? Is it his father? Or perhaps his father has been killed. The ambiguity makes the boy seem painfully vulnerable. I fear he trusts the adult, the soldier, too readily, too completely. That he will be turned into a soldier or ruthlessly killed like thousands of other children have been. Yet in his innocent reaching out, in his attempt to hold onto something, he reveals that hope is possible in the face of fear, the deep, twisting root of war.

The photo always leaves me with a question: Why is it so hard to listen to what children know?

A week after the 9/11 attacks, I took Tessa to Chinatown for lunch. On the way home I was listening to the radio. I thought she was reading *Tom Sawyer* in the back seat. "They're not 'events,' Daddy!" she said suddenly. "What?" I asked, bewildered. "They're not just 'events,'" she said. "What do you mean?" I asked, baffled. "That man on the radio keeps talking about the 'events' of September 11, but they're not."

"What are they?" I asked.

"They're something else," she said. "Something, very, very sad." Tears welled in her eyes, and then mine. We came up with some substitute words for September 11: a horrible day, a sad day, a dark day, a lonely day, a lost day.

As we cruised home from Chinatown I watched Tessa in the rearview mirror. She stared intently out the back window at the Chicago skyline, at the irregular pattern of buildings jutting into an infinite, pale blue sky. What could she be thinking? I wanted to say something, something reassuring. But then, for some reason, I reached over and pushed the little button that autolocks all the car doors. I craned back over the seat to check her lap belt, to be sure it was in the right position and fastened tight. I checked my speed and eased my foot off the accelerator. Bewildered by the knot of anxiety tightening in my stomach, I took a deep breath. "I've got to slow down," I thought to myself, still unsure what Tessa was telling me.

Word

The world is God's language to us.
The universe is the Word of God.

—SIMONE WEIL[8]

Carol and I wake just before dawn in the farmhouse bunkroom and tiptoe barefoot downstairs, careful not to wake the kids. We are here for the weekend. Summer is over, and school starts Monday. Life will accelerate. So we both savor the quiet time to read and write and talk. We make coffee and loosely plan out the day. Then she sits down on the porch to read the *New Yorker,* and I grab my laptop and walk over to the henhouse. After plugging in the computer, I sit down at my desk and stare off into the woods. And it hits me: I've been doing this for over a year now. A year. But in spite of all the hours sitting here waiting I'm not sure what I've learned. I don't know if I'm a better father or husband or writer or teacher. I hope I've gotten a bit better at prayer, at making myself sit here, at listening to silence.

A line from my seeds file: "The silence of God is God."[9] Poet Carolyn Forché's provocative sentence gets me wondering if true silence is even possible. Where would one experience the complete absence of sound? Or maybe she means the complete absence of love? I check the reference and remember the context: she was writing about Jews hiding during the holocaust—about how/when/if God's silence could be "heard" as a kind of presence in a desperate situation. I can't imagine the depth of that silence. What could it say?

I keep listening.

The sun breaks the night open. A mourning dove flutters from its perch on a cottonwood. I feel overwhelmed, top-heavy—like the huge sunflower whose head became so laden with seeds that it toppled over in the garden yesterday. It took its ten-foot stalk with it, nearly pulling up its own roots. Abby and Tessa laid the flower head out to dry in the sun. They want to feed it to Pippy, their gerbil.

My head is heavy because it is full of thoughts that are not related to my topic. And *that* is the real problem—I have a topic: the relationship between words and the Word, between the art of writing and the art of faith.

Over the years a stack of rejection letters has taught me that if you use the capitalized word "God" in an essay, you'll have a hard time placing it in a literary journal. If you use the phrase "Word of God," (i.e., the experience or manifestation of God), you can forget it. In literary nonfiction these terms suggest "narrow" thinking that will taint the writer's art. This is true to a degree. "God" is an idea that is usually aligned with doctrine and religion. But God is also undefinable, irreducible. Words are only a symbolic approximation of reality. Perhaps the problem is that "God" connotes so much that it denotes nothing at all. Most of the nature writers I admire approach the idea of God with inclusive, neutral substitutes. They still choose huge abstract nouns: "spirit" or "source," or a capitalized word like Nature or Mystery. But these words are not so historically and politically charged as God, nor as easy to manipulate.

As a missionary in the early 1990s at a little college in the Philippines, I taught English and literature classes. But once I taught a theology class, and I asked my students to write a one-sentence response to the question "What is God?"

Some of the students gave predictably vague responses: "God is my rock and redeemer"; "God is love"; "God is spirit"; "God is the source of all things"; or "God is what we ultimately trust." (We had just read Paul Tillich.)

But I was most intrigued by the concrete responses that stemmed from pieces of everyday life: "God is like the rain that falls"; "God is rice"; or "God is my family gathered at dinner." All the responses had similar implications: *God is what sustains us.* Yet the responses that attempted to limit the infinite to finite concrete nouns again reminded me of how writing is like faith. Both attempt to bridge the known and unknown. Both are metaphorical.

God cannot be explained by a writer nor by any work of art, only revealed. The revelation of Word is beyond, and yet within words.

"The sun shines without vocabulary," writes the essayist Scott Russell Sanders. "The salmon has no name for the urge that drives it upstream. The newborn groping for the nipple knows hunger long before it knows a single word. Even with an entire dictionary in one's head, one eventually comes to the end of words. Then what? Then drink deep like the baby, swim like the salmon, burn like any brief star."[10]

This helps. By defining the limits of words, I can better imagine the idea of Word, that creation itself has its own language.

But I'm starting to feel like the sunflower again. I walk outside to clear my head. After a few steps I see something I've noticed before but not examined: a dried leaf floating in mid-air, seemingly suspended four feet off the ground by absolutely nothing. I look closer. It is a wild grape leaf, and Japanese Beetles have eaten away all the flesh, leaving a brittle spine and a complex network of veins that make odd, lovely shadows on the ground below it. What happened? The beetles ate the leaf while it was still on a vine somewhere. A gust of wind freed it to drift into a single strand of spider web spun between a dogwood and a tulip tree. I look, but I can't find the spider on either end of its high wire.

The quivering leaf filigree and its shadow are a masterpiece that cannot be reproduced with words or paint or quarter notes. But who or what then is the artist?

I return to the henhouse and my topic: words and Word. It has interested me for a long time, in part because after I finished my undergraduate work, I did two M.A. degrees back to back, first in creative writing and then in religion. I wrote a collection of essays about the Nicaraguan revolution and the split in the Catholic Church. As a young graduate student who had spent most of his life in Iowa,

I found those months living in Nicaragua an arresting introduction to the "two-thirds" world and to U.S. foreign policy. Though the stakes were lower because I couldn't be drafted, the war in Nicaragua became my Vietnam—the public historical event as personal moral dilemma that required a response. My time there was transformative. The more I experienced the creative and courageous faith of the Nicaraguan people, the more I began to question my own and to wonder about the relationship between the art of words and the art of Word. After I finished writing the book I went to seminary.

The kids sleep late. It is midmorning when the screen door slaps. Tessa and Abby come in carrying two tin saucepans and a large plastic cup for blackberry picking. "Hi, Daddy. We found you!" They smile, rub the sleep out of their eyes, and give me the cup. Most of the blackberry bushes are along the meadow on the other side of the creek—a ten-minute walk. We start out. Bennett and Carol are gathering lettuce in the garden and will meet us later.

The entrance to the main path near the henhouse leads into a green tunnel that feels like it will take you to Narnia, as if it were beyond the reach of time. A hundred feet ahead, the path bends into the darkness. The grass and pine needle floor is dappled with shimmering yellow patches that keep shifting, mirroring how the sunlight finds its way through the blowing canopy of pine and oak branches. The magical twinkling lights on the path make it look as though it's alive. After awhile, it seems the light is coming from within the earth rather than from above, like the spirit of the earth itself is breaking through. The walls on either side are thick stands of chest-high goldenrod and thistle, as tall as Abby. As we walk, we startle creatures out of the weeds; a deer breaks across the path, then a rabbit. Some wild turkeys explode into flight in the distance.

When we are in the middle of the woods, I tell Tessa and Abby about having to memorize Robert Frost's "The Road Not Taken," in seventh grade. The poem has since become one of the most hackneyed metaphors in American literature, but the image still matters to me, and I often think of it while walking our trails. I try to recite it for the girls and screw up the third stanza. But Abby says she likes it anyway.

As a kid I didn't consider that Frost's road might be "life," nor the connotations of a "fork in the road." But even then, when I read the part about where the road "bent in the undergrowth," I knew what it meant. Though I couldn't articulate it, I deeply felt the implications. I saw the mysterious bends and turns on all the trails and roads I had already walked, that place where the path disappeared and could only be imagined, a point of both ending and beginning.

Frost's words, his simple image, connected me to something bigger, even when I was twelve. Poetry often does this for me (more so than prose), because of its intellectual and emotional density. The poet saturates imagery with meaning. The human brain can hold around 30,000 separate words, but the poet only needs a handful to reveal the essence of human *being*. Poets answer life's questions with a ripe Loring peach and a rusty red wheelbarrow and a squawking bluejay. Yet despite their preoccupation with details, they get at the heart of things. They shape words into moments that recreate the holy. They have helped me understand how words and Word are related, and how prayer can be a bridge between them.

"Poetry like prayer is a dialogue with the sacred," writes Kathleen Norris.[11]

From William Wordsworth to Emily Dickinson to Annie Dillard, many poets have entered both conversations. (Or perhaps it is the same one?) Like Norris, they see writing as a spiritual discipline, as a rare quality of attention. This kind of attentiveness is both a state of reverence or awe, and an emptying, a deep listening—for the relatedness of one thing to all things. It is an attempt to become radically permeable to the whole of creation, to spin a fragile web of words that might somehow catch Word.

When we arrive at the meadow, large clusters of blackberries are pulling their branches down onto the path. About half are ripe. Tessa and Abby, who have been bickering about who can rightfully identify a poison ivy plant, stop when they see the berries and run to pick them. The ripe ones are huge, as big as the last joint of my thumb. Abby eats the first handful she picks and then puts one in her pan. Tessa picks a handful, puts them in her pan, and then tries one. The berries are remarkably sweet. Soon I notice that both of the girls are squatting in a patch of poison ivy while picking the lower berries on the back side of a bush.

When they finally scramble out of the thicket and have unsnagged the last berry branch from their shirts, their little pans are about a quarter full. They know that their arms are scratched, but not that their lips and cheeks are stained with bright purple juice. Tessa wants to know who has picked the most. I say I can't tell, but it's clear that all our berries will fit into one pan. So we dump them all into hers.

About this time Carol and Bennett come slowly plodding down the trail. He is ecstatic to see the girls and starts doing a little jig. Then he grabs a fist full of the tender berries from the pan and squeezes them into jam.

"Nooooo!" Abby screams, as if someone has just murdered her pet cat. Bennett looks delighted. Tessa grabs his hand and leads him to a bush and helps him pick a few berries. This distracts him and satisfies his curiosity. Soon he's ready to walk back.

On the way home Carol and I walk behind the kids, who keep running ahead and circling back to us with sticks and leaves, like sparrows building a nest in a moving tree. When we all emerge from the overgrown path, the sun is flooding the grassy yard around the farmhouse. Tessa and Abby run for the swings that hang from two huge silver maples. The swings are 1-foot squares of plywood with a hole drilled in the middle. A 25-foot length of knotted rope runs through the hole up to a high limb. The girls jump onto the dangling wooden seats, tighten their legs around the rope, and wait for me to push them. I run them each as high as I can and let go to their roller-coaster screams. Excited, Bennett runs at them to get closer to the action. Carol follows and scoops him up before he is knocked over like a bowling pin. The three of us sit down on the warm blanket of light and watch Tessa and Abby's swinging bodies: two laughing and waving pendulums rising and falling over the earth, in and out of shadow and sunshine. I am lost in the prayer, in the wonder of gravity and wind and maple trees.

And the only words I have left are *thank you.*

A Brief History of
"The Covenant Farm"

—NANCY JONES, SAWYER, MICHIGAN

We purchased "The Farm," where much of this book takes place, in 1980. Al Pitcher, an ethics professor at The University of Chicago and a member of our church, envisioned a rural extension of the intentional faith community he was helping to form in Chicago, the Covenantal Community of University Church. An environmentalist, he sought a place for a group to grow their own food, retreat from city stress, get in touch with the seasons, and build community. We found a forty-five–acre plot of land with an old henhouse and a stone farmhouse that fire had left in ruins. The whole place had been abandoned for three years.

We worked off and on for ten years before the stone farmhouse was inhabitable. Al recruited families who were looking for a project, not a weekend vacation. During those years, we lived in out-buildings and used tents for our weekend visits, which centered around never-ending fix-up projects, communal gardens, trips to the beach, and long games of canasta. In the late 1980s, when the productivity of the farmland we rented to our neighbor diminished, a farm member discovered a free county reforestation program that would plant thousands of pine and hardwood over thirty acres. The trees were planted, and thus we began to witness the land's restoration. Today our woods, now with a maze of walking trails, bring us great joy. Wildlife has returned to the area, and a lucky day will bring encounters with not only deer and rabbit, but coyote and wild turkey, fox and blue heron.

Our community consists of seven family units who make decisions for maintenance and improvements and share expenses, providing us with the luxury of a getaway that none of us could afford alone. And our collective labor has not only made the place more comfortable but also has created a deep sense of community. Over the years the life of the farm has become intertwined with the lives of our families. The land has nurtured a sapling planted to mark the birth of a child, the celebration of a couple's marriage, and the laughter and discoveries of our children, and has received the ashes of two of our members who have died.

When I think of the farm now, I think of my husband, Dan, and I, so many years ago, pulling into the driveway, climbing out into the waist-high weeds, and tramping over to the henhouse, where our friend Al was sweeping up. The place was ankle deep in rusty nails, chain, and pieces of machinery I didn't recognize—remnants from what had once been a farm. Not knowing exactly how to help or where to begin, we made our way through the piles of junk to the end of the building, where Al was standing. He had cleaned out an eight-by-eight-foot square amid the junk pile and arranged some chairs for us. We sat and looked out on the cornfield in back—our cornfield, our land. Yes, this was the property, forty-five acres, that he had convinced us and several other families to purchase together. The place was a wreck, but that's not what Al saw. That day he saw our junk-filled henhouse as "a room with a view." With his back to the rusted nails and tractor parts, he looked out at the field and mused, "Just look at the possibilities."

To this day my favorite spot remains a chair in the henhouse where I often sit on summer mornings. The view has changed a bit, but I still watch the world in wonder and ponder the possibilities.

Notes

AUTUMN

[1]Gretel Ehrlich, *The Solace of Open Spaces* (New York: Viking, 1985), 130.

[2]Walt Whitman, *Whitman: Poetry and Prose* (New York: Library of America, 1982), 85 (from *Leaves of Grass*, first published in 1855).

[3]Simone Weil, *Notebooks*, trans. A. F. Wills (New York: G. P. Putnam and Sons, 1956).

[4]Huston Smith, *Why Religion Matters* (San Francisco: HarperCollins, 2001), 138.

[5]Noah ben Shea, *Jacob the Baker* (New York: Villard, 1989), 51.

[6]E.L. Doctorow, quoted in Anne Lamott, *Bird by Bird: Some Instructions on Writing and Life* (New York: Anchor Books/Doubleday, 1995), 18.

[7]Kurt Vonnegut quoted in ibid., 32.

[8]Leonard Cohen, excerpt of lyric from his song "Anthem," from the album *The Future,* A and M Records, 1992.

[9]Louise Erdrich, *The Blue Jay's Dance* (New York: HarperCollins, 1995), 41.

[10]Sarton's essay is reprinted in *Guidelines: A Cross-Cultural Reading/Writing Text* (Cambridge: Cambridge University Press, 1999), 37–39.

[11]Li-Young Lee, "Nativity," in *Book of My Nights* (Rochester, N.Y.: BOA, 2001), 10.

[12]Patti Ann Rogers, *The Dream of the Marsh Wren: Writing as Reciprocal Creation* (Minneapolis: Milkweed, 1999), 7.

[13]Ibid., 91.

[14]Wendell Berry in an interview with Anne Husted Burleigh, "Wendell Berry's Community," *Crisis* 18, no. 1 (January, 2000): 28–33.

[15]Mary Oliver, "The Summer Day," *New and Selected Poems* (Boston: Beacon Press, 1992).

[16]Annie Dillard, *Holy the Firm* (New York: Harper and Row, 1977), 71–72.

[17]Emily Dickinson, "Death Is a Dialogue between," *The Complete Poems of Emily Dickinson* (New York: Little Brown, 1960), 480.

[18]Walt Whitman, *Whitman: Poetry and Prose* (New York: Library of America, 1982), 217 (from 1891 version of *Leaves of Grass,* section 31).

[19]From study by the Mouse Genome Sequencing Consortium, published in the Dec. 5, 2002 issue of *Nature* magazine.

WINTER

[1]Dorothee Soelle, *Death by Bread Alone* (Philadelphia: Fortress Press, 1978), 71.

[2]Annie Dillard, *Holy the Firm* (New York: Harper and Row, 1977), 61.

[3]Neil Postman, *Technopoly: The Surrender of Culture to Technology* (New York: Random House, 1993), 14–15.

[4]Dorothy Day, quoted in Robert Coles, *The Spiritual Life of Children* (Boston: Houghton Mifflin, 1990), 329.

[5]Mary McCarthy, *On the Contrary* (New York: Octagon Books, 1976), 121.

[6]John Modschiedler, "Understanding Violence" in *Liberation and Ethics: Essays in Religious Social Ethics in Honor of Gibson Winter,* ed. Charles Amjad-Ali and W. Alvin Pitcher (Chicago: Center for the Scientific Study of Religion, 1985), 193–203.

[7]Our professor had a twenty-year-long relationship with the elders on this reservation and powerfully modeled the cross-cultural respect and humility she expected of all her students. This, I assume, is why she was always invited back with her students.

[8]Wendell Berry, "The Design of a House," in *The Selected Poems of Wendell Berry* (Washington, D.C.: Counterpoint Press, 1999), 11.

[9]Anne Lamott, *Operating Instructions: A Journal of My Son's First Year* (New York: Fawcett, 1993), 161.

[10]Ibid., 161

[11]Ibid., 97

[12]Anne Lamott, *Traveling Mercies: Some Thoughts on Faith* (New York: Pantheon, 1999), 168.

[13]Anne Lamott, *Bird by Bird: Some Instructions on Writing and Life* (New York: Anchor, 1995), 32.

[14]Marvin Bell, "To Dorothy," *Nightworks: Poems 1962–2000* (Port Townsend, Wash.: Copper Canyon Press, 2000).

[15]Lamott, *Bird by Bird*, 13.

SPRING

[1]Maria Ranier Rilke, *Letters to a Young Poet* (New York: W.W. Norton, 1993), 30.

[2]Wendell Berry, *What Are People For?* (New York: North Point Press, 1990), 210.

[3]For further discussion see Augustine, "On Miracles," in *City of God,* book 22, chapters 8–10.

[4]E. B. White, *Charlotte's Web* (New York: Harper Collins, 1952), 109.

[5]Ibid., 171.

[6]The words *humus* and *human* share the same root as *humble*.

[7]White, *Charlotte's Web*, 183.

[8]*Tao Te Ching,* trans. Stephen Mitchell (New York: Harper Collins, 1999), chapter 44.

[9]See the first chapter of David Myers's *The American Paradox: Spiritual Hunger in an Age of Plenty* (New Haven, Conn.: Yale Univ. Press, 2000).

[10]Rabindranath Tagore, *A Tagore Reader,* ed. Amiya Chakravarty (Boston: Beacon, 1966), 286.

[11]Though Kierkegaard saw this leap as the "third stage" of life, after his progression through aesthetics and ethics, the hierarchy seems odd to me, given that all three parts of a person seem equally important.

[12]Rilke, *Letters to a Young Poet,* 35.

[13]Wendell Berry, "Christianity and the Survival of Creation," *Crosscurrents* 43, no. 2 (Summer 1993): 152.

SUMMER

[1]Henry David Thoreau, *Walden* (New York: W.W. Norton, 1951), 22.

[2]Excerpted from Jim Moore, "9/11/01" (first two stanzas), available online at. http://www.loft.org/BeyondWords11.htm, Web site of The Loft Literary Center (Minneapolis).

[3]James Richardson, *Interglacial: New and Selected Poems and Aphorisms* (Keene, N.Y.: Ausable Press, 2004), 224.

[4]Peg Kehret, *Small Steps: The Year I Got Polio* (Morton Grove, Ill.: Albert Whitman & Co., 1996).

[5]Ibid., 67.

[6]Thomas Merton, *The Hidden Ground of Love*, ed. William Shannon (New York: Farrar, Straus, Giroux, 1985), 294–95.

[7]Meister Eckhart, quoted in F. Lynn Bachelda, *Canticles of the Earth* (Chicago: Loyola Press, 2004), 92.

[8]Simone Weil, *Notebooks,* trans. A. F. Wills (New York: G. P. Putnam's Sons, 1956), 480.

[9]Carolyn Forché, *The Angel of History* (New York: Harper Collins, 1994), 5.

[10]Scott Russell Sanders, *Staying Put: Making a Home in a Restless World* (Boston: Beacon Press, 1993), 194.

[11]Katheen Norris, *The Cloister Walk* (New York: Riverhead, 1996), 64.